FEMALE TARS

ℱEMALE TARS

Women Aboard Ship in the Age of Sail

SUZANNE J. STARK

NAVAL INSTITUTE PRESS   ANNAPOLIS, MARYLAND

Library of Congress Cataloging-in-Publication Data
Stark, Suzanne J., 1926–
Female tars: women aboard ship in the age of sail / Suzanne J. Stark.
p.   cm.
Includes bibliographical references (p.   ) and index.
ISBN 1-55750-738-4 (cloth: alk. paper)
1. Great Britain. Royal Navy—Women—History—18th century.
2. Great Britain. Royal Navy—Women—History—19th century. I. Title.
VB325. G7S73   1996
359'. 0082—dc20

Printed in the United States of America on acid-free paper ∞

96 97 98 99 00 01 02 03   9 8 7 6 5 4 3 2
First printing

First two verses from "A Man of War Song No 56," *A Sailors Songbag:
An American Rebel in an English Prison, 1777–1779*, ed. George G. Carey
(Amherst: University of Massachusetts Press, 1976), 147.
Reprinted by permission of the publisher.

Two verses from "The Maiden Sailor" by John Curtin, *The Pepys Ballads*, ed.,
Hyder Edward Rollins, 8 vols. (Cambridge: Harvard University Press, 1932),
6: 176–77. Reprinted by permission of the publisher.

Illustration on title page: Detail of a line engraving by C. Mosley. From
Charles N. Robinson, *The British Tar in Fact and Fiction* (New York and London:
Harper and Brothers, 1909). Boston Athenaeum.

CONTENTS

ILLUSTRATIONS

ACKNOWLEDGMENTS

I WOULD LIKE TO ACKNOWLEDGE the generosity of my daughter Francesca Macdonald Stark, whose incisive suggestions helped me to clarify my evolving theses throughout many years of research.

I am indebted to my friends Jeanne Steig, Leslie Larkin, and Kenneth Kronenberg, who read a series of revisions and offered wise counsel. Three English friends—John Braun, Claire Ritchie, and Bridget Spiers—took time from their own projects to fill gaps in my research in British archives.

I also am beholden to James Feeney and the other staff members of the Boston Athenaeum, where a great part of my research was done, for tracking down many obscure sources.

Mary V. Yates, my editor, worked miracles in organizing my convoluted syntax and saved me many embarrassing errors.

The extensive quotations from the autobiography of Mary Lacy in chapter 4 are reproduced courtesy of the Trustees of the Boston Public Library. I copied these passages from the very rare volume *The History of the Female Shipwright* (London: M. Lewis, 1773) in their Rare Book Room. My transcribing was done some years ago with a pencil (pens are not allowed in the room, and rightly so). It took many long days, but I enjoyed the process. Since the book is now on microfilm, the actual volume is no longer available for study. This preserves the original and brings the material to a wider audience, but I am glad I got to use the real thing.

FEMALE TARS

Introduction

"For quarter, for quarter," the Spanish lads did cry,
"No quarter, no quarter," this damsel did reply;
"You've had the best of quarter that I can well afford,
You must fight, sink, or swim, my boys, or jump overboard."

So now the battle's over, we'll drink a can of wine,
And you will drink to your love, and I will drink to mine;
Good health unto the damsel who fought upon the main,
And here's to the royal ship, the Rainbow by name.

—"As We Were A-Sailing"

THE BRITISH ROYAL NAVY in the Age of Sail—ruler of the waves and protector of the world's largest empire—has always been accounted a strictly male preserve, Britain's strongest bastion of male exclusivity. The belief was ancient and ubiquitous that women had no place at sea. They not only were weak, hysterical, and feckless and distracted the men from their duties, but they also brought bad luck to the ships they traveled in; they called forth supernatural winds that sank the vessels and drowned the men.

Despite this superstitious prohibition, there were women living and working in naval ships from the late seventeenth century to the middle of the nineteenth, although their presence on board was officially ignored and even hidden.

It was not until 1993 that Great Britain, following the lead of other countries including the United States, integrated women into the regular navy as full-fledged sailors. Officially, women were first brought into the Royal Navy in 1917, but only as an auxiliary force: the Women's Royal Naval Service. The Wrens were recruited to release men from shore duty; in fact, their peculiar motto was "Never at Sea." In 1919, at the close of World War I, the Wrens were disbanded, but in 1938 they were reinstituted and proved their prowess and courage from World War II up to 1993. Although in 1990 some Wrens were assigned to sea duty, they continued to be, as they had always been, denied many of the responsibilities, opportunities, and benefits offered by the regular service. To cite one odd example, Wren officers' uniforms were without the gold braid used on the uniforms of the regular naval officers. Gold was deemed too expensive for use by a women's auxiliary.

The idea of women serving in the navy has always been resisted. A *Times* (London) article of 2 November 1993, issued on the day the Wrens were incorporated into the regular navy, noted, "The Wrens have always suffered from a public image problem. For nearly 80 years...as far as the public was concerned, the girls in navy blue were either frustrated lesbians or uniformed nymphomaniacs attempting to splice not only the mainbrace but also every petty officer aboard."[1] Few of the people who today are opposed to women serving in naval ships are aware of the three-hundred-year-old tradition of women living on board. The sea service of women of earlier centuries was, of course, very different from that of the women in the twentieth-century navy. Women on board naval ships in the Age of Sail played a variety of widely divergent roles that divide into three main categories, discussed in the first three chapters of this book.

The largest category was composed of the hundreds of prostitutes who shared the quarters of the crew on the lower deck whenever a ship was in port. To understand why the navy unofficially condoned this practice, and to discover what led the prostitutes to this appalling fate, requires not only knowledge of naval history but awareness of the situation of women in the society as a whole.

Second, there were the wives of warrant officers, many of whom spent years at sea; the ship was often their only home. These women were active participants in battle, nursing the wounded and carrying powder to the guns. They too were ignored by the Admiralty; their names were not entered on the ships' books, and they received no pay and no food rations. (Wives, daughters, and guests of captains and admirals also traveled in naval ships, but their reasons for going to sea were different, and so were their experiences on board. Their role is not discussed in this book.)

The third group was composed of women in male disguise who actually served in naval crews or as marines. Reports of such women have always titillated the public, but no one, including the women's own officers, took them seriously once their true gender was discovered. Accounts of their exploits were embellished with themes from a popular genre of fiction in which the heroine goes to sea to find her lost lover. No one tried very hard to answer difficult questions about the real female tars, questions such as what induced them to join the navy when most of the men in naval crews had to be forced on board by press gangs.[2]

The final chapter of this book is devoted to the autobiography of the redoubtable woman seaman and shipwright Mary Lacy, who served in the Royal Navy for twelve years. Her detailed account of her life in the navy during and following the Seven Years' War provides insights into the reasons why women such as she joined the navy and were so determined to continue to serve despite severe hardships, insights impossible to come to from the other meager sources available.

The primary aims of this study are to disentangle myth from fact in the stories of the women who lived on the lower deck of the ships of the sailing navy, to discover why these women chose to participate in the harsh life on board, and to place them within the social context of the limited roles open to lower-class British women in the eighteenth and early nineteenth centuries.

I have modernized the spelling and punctuation of contemporary quotations except in a few instances where the original form provides special insight into the culture of the time.

CHAPTER 1

Prostitutes and Seamen's Wives on Board in Port

*Now our ship is arrived
And anchored in Plymouth Sound.
We'll drink a health to the Whores
That does our ship surround.*

*Then into the boat they gett
And alongside they come.
"Waterman, call my Husband,
For I'm damb'd if I know his name."*

—"A Man of War Song"

IN A LETTER DATED 19 April 1666 to Samuel Pepys, at that time clerk of the acts, Admiral John Mennes, comptroller of the British Royal Navy, complained that the ships of the navy "are pestered with women." "There are," wrote Mennes, "as many petticoats as breeches" on board, and, he added, the women remain in the vessels "for weeks together."[1]

Naval chaplain Henry Teonge described the scene he witnessed in the frigate *Assistance* in 1675 on the night she entered the Thames estuary on her way from London to Dover:

Our ship was that night well furnished but ill manned, few of them [the seamen] being well able to keep watch had there been occasion. You would have wondered to see here a man and a woman creep into a hammock, the woman's legs to the hams hanging over the sides or out at the end of it. Another couple sleeping on a chest; others kissing and clipping [hugging], half drunk, half sober, or rather half asleep.[2]

A hundred and thirty years later, the scene on board had not changed. Whenever a naval ship came into port, hundreds of women, most of them prostitutes, joined the men on the already crowded lower deck and remained until the vessel put to sea. The seaman William Robinson, who served in the Royal Navy from 1805 to 1811, described the arrival of his ship at Portsmouth, England:

After having moored our ship, swarms of boats came round us...and a great many of them were freighted with cargoes of ladies, a sight that was truly gratifying, and a great treat, for our crew, consisting of six hundred and upwards, nearly all young men, had seen but one woman on board for eighteen months.... In the course of the afternoon, we had about four hundred and fifty [women] on board.

Of all the human race, these poor young creatures are the most pitiable; the ill-usage and the degradation they are driven to submit to are indescribable; but from habit they become callous, indifferent as to delicacy of speech and behavior, and so totally lost to all sense of shame that they seem to retain no quality which properly belongs to women but the shape and name....

On the arrival of any man of war in port, these girls flock down to the shore where boats are always ready.... Old Charon [the boatman who carries the women out to the ships] often refuses to take some of them, observing to one that she is *too old*, to another that she is *too ugly*, and that he shall not be able to *sell* them.... The only apology that can be made for the savage conduct of these unfeeling brutes is that they run a chance of not

being permitted to carry a cargo alongside unless it makes a
good show-off; for it has been often known that, on approach-
ing a ship, the officer in command has so far forgot himself as to
order the Waterman to push off—that he should not bring such
a cargo of d——d ugly devils on board, and that he would not
allow any of his men to have them.... Here the Waterman is a
loser, for he takes them conditionally; that is, if they are made
choice of, or what he calls *sold*, he receives three shillings each;
and, if not, then no pay.... Thus these poor unfortunates are
taken to market like cattle, and whilst this system is observed, it
cannot with truth be said that the slave trade is abolished in
England.[3]

While Robinson and other seamen expressed their pity for the
prostitutes, commissioned officers, from their isolated vantage
point high on the quarterdeck above the fray of the lower deck,
showed little sympathy for the unfortunate women, accepting their
presence on board as an unsavory but necessary situation.

Horatio Nelson's noted rapport with his men did not extend to
their women, or at least not to their temporary women. He wrote
to Admiral John Jervis in 1801, "I hope there will be orders to complete our complement, and the ship to be paid on Saturday. On
Sunday we shall get rid of all the women, dogs, and pigeons, and
on Wednesday, with the lark, I hope to be under sail for Torbay."[4]

Even the nineteenth-century reformer Admiral Edward Hawker,
who first brought the situation of the prostitutes to public attention, was concerned only with getting the women out of the ships,
not with improving their lot. A pamphlet that Hawker published
anonymously in 1821 presents a highly colored but not inaccurate
picture of a naval ship in port in the period following the Napoleonic Wars:

The whole of the shocking, disgraceful transactions of the lower
deck is impossible to describe—the dirt, filth, and stench...and
where, in bed (each man being allowed only sixteen inches
breadth for his hammock) they [each pair] are squeezed

W. Elmes, "Exporting Cattle, Not Insurable." A bumboat carries prostitutes out to a naval ship. Note the stereotyped depiction of the women as fat, old, and ugly. In fact a large percentage of ship's prostitutes were undernourished and very young. NATIONAL MARITIME MUSEUM, GREENWICH, LONDON

between the next hammocks and must be witnesses of each other's actions.

It is frequently the case that men take two prostitutes on board at a time, so that sometimes there are more women than men on board.... Men and women are turned by hundreds into one compartment, and in sight and hearing of each other, shamelessly and unblushingly couple like dogs.

Let those who have never seen a ship of war picture to themselves a very large low room (hardly capable of holding the men) with five hundred men and probably three hundred or four hundred women of the vilest description shut up in it, and giving way to every excess of debauchery that the grossest passions of human nature can lead them to, and they see the deck of a seventy-four-gun ship the night of her arrival in port.[5]

The Scene in Port, at Home and Abroad

It is difficult for us today, familiar as we are with the order and discipline of modern naval vessels, to realize what pandemonium existed in the sailing ships of the Royal Navy anchored in Portsmouth, Plymouth, and other naval ports.

Not only did hundreds of women share the lower deck with the seamen. There were also children of all ages, from toddlers brought on board by the seamen's wives to adolescent boys in the crew who frolicked around the decks where the crowds of men and women were drinking, dancing, and fornicating. The tradesmen, always referred to as "the Jews," and the bumboat men and women, whose boats brought merchandise out to the ships, set up stalls on board and hawked their wares among the crowds as they would in a marketplace on land.[6] They sold, on credit until payday, fresh fruit, clothes, trinkets, and any other items that a sailor back from a long voyage would fancy—including liquor, which they, like the prostitutes, smuggled on board. Dogs, cats, parrots, and other pets added to the general disorder.[7] The fifty-gun *Salisbury* returned to England from Newfoundland in the 1780s with seventy-five dogs on board, approximately one for every four men.[8] At night, when the hammocks were up and sleep had overcome the crowd, a cacophony of snores issued from hundreds of throats, made more sonorous by the great quantity of liquor imbibed throughout the day.

Officers became so inured to the presence of large numbers of prostitutes in their ships that the women were not always sent on shore even when a ship was inspected by a royal visitor; they were merely hidden away. The seaman William Richardson tells of the visit of Princess Caroline to H.M.S. *Caesar* during which the princess not only caught a glimpse of "the girls" but actually acknowledged them:

> On May 11, 1806, Her Royal Highness Caroline, consort to His
> Royal Highness George, Prince of Wales [later, King George IV]

…paid our Admiral [Sir Richard Strachan] a visit on board the *Caesar,* accompanied by Lady Hood and some others of distinction, and were received with a royal salute of twenty-one guns. The ship had been cleaned and repaired for the purpose, and all the girls (some hundreds) on board were ordered to keep below on the orlop deck [far in the depths of the vessel] and out of sight until the visit was over.

As Her Royal Highness was going round the decks and viewing the interior, she cast her eyes down the main hatchway, and there saw a number of the girls peeping up at her.[9]

Princess Caroline was not one to avoid causing a little public embarrassment if it amused her to do so. Although Richardson may have improvised on her actual words, there is no reason to doubt that the situation was much as he described it:

"Sir Richard," she said, "you told me there were no women on board the ship, but I am convinced there are, as I have seen them peeping up from that place, and am inclined to think they are put down there on my account. I therefore request that it may no longer be permitted."

So when Her Royal Highness had got on the quarterdeck again the girls were set at liberty, and up they came like a flock of sheep, and the booms and gangway were soon covered with them, staring at the Princess as if she had been a being just dropped from the clouds.[10]

Crowds of women came on board Royal Navy vessels in foreign harbors, too. In West Indian ports it was customary for officers to arrange with plantation owners to send large groups of slaves—black female field hands—to their ships. Captain Edward Thompson's description of the scene in ships at Antigua in the 1750s reveals the attitudes of officers of his day: "Bad smells don't hurt the sailor's appetite, each man possessing a temporary lady whose

Woodcut from a nineteenth-century broadside ballad. The woman is probably a West Indian field hand provided by a plantation owner who had a contract with the ship's officers to send women on board. From John Ashton, ed., *Real Sailor-Songs* (London: Leadenhall, 1891), 49.

pride is her constancy to the man she chooses. I have known 350 women sup and sleep on board on a Sunday evening and return at daybreak to their different plantations."[11] It seems most unlikely that the women had any part in the choice of whom they slept with, and as for bad smells, they could not have smelled worse than the men, who had been cooped up in their stifling ship for months with few if any baths or changes of clothing. Even when a seaman was taken with the urge to bathe, his only bathing facility was a bucket of cold seawater. There were no uniforms for seamen; they had to provide their own clothing, and many a man had only the clothes he was wearing when he first came on board. When a seaman got around to doing his laundry, also in a bucket of salt water, he first bleached it in urine, which was collected in a large barrel for this purpose.

In 1788 Prince William Henry (later crowned William IV), when in command of the thirty-two-gun *Andromeda* at Jamaica, included the following instructions in his orders to his officers: "Order the 8th, requesting and directing the first lieutenant or commanding officer to see all strangers out of his Majesty's ship under my command at gun-fire [sunset] is by no means meant to restrain the officers and men from having either black or white women on board through the night so long as the discipline is unhurt by the indulgence."[12] Even after 1833, when slavery was abolished in the British West Indies, officers continued to arrange for female plantation workers to come into their ships. As late as the 1840s a frigate captain at Barbados ordered his first lieutenant to secure a black woman for every man and boy in his crew.[13]

The navies of other countries also took prostitutes on board in foreign ports. While the U.S.S. *Dolphin,* the first United States warship to go to Hawaii, was at Honolulu in 1826, her commander, Lieutenant John Percival, learned that the governor of the island of Oahu had been induced by the leader of the Protestant missionaries to issue an order that women should no longer be allowed to go for immoral purposes on board vessels anchored there. Percival was furious. Since women had been allowed on board the British frigate *Blonde,* under the command of Captain the Right Honorable George Anson, Lord Byron, when she visited Honolulu the previous year, Percival, a touchy man, viewed this ruling as a personal insult and an attack on the honor of the United States Navy. He announced that he would not leave the islands until women were allowed to go on board the *Dolphin.* "I would," he declared, "rather have my hands tied or even cut off and be carried home maimed as a criminal than to have it said that Lord Byron was allowed a privilege greater than was allowed me." The governor rescinded the order for the duration of the *Dolphin's* visit, and even the mission school was emptied of girls, who were rowed out to the *Dolphin* amid the happy shouts of her crew.[14]

WHY PROSTITUTES WERE ALLOWED ON BOARD

Why did the Royal Navy for so many centuries permit hundreds of prostitutes to live in its ships? The sad truth is that a great percentage of seamen were taken into the navy against their will, forced on board by press gangs. Living conditions were terrible, and pay was both meager and slow in coming. If men were given shore leave, they deserted. Therefore, once a seaman was brought on board, he might not get out until his vessel was decommissioned, and commissions usually extended three to five years, often even longer on foreign stations. He also might be transferred from one ship to another with no leave between the two.[15]

Naval vessels were anchored far from shore, and the men were not encouraged to learn to swim. In addition to the marine patrols on board, some captains even went so far as to have special guard boats circling their ships throughout the night to prevent seamen from slipping away under cover of darkness. Dr. Samuel Johnson, the eighteenth-century lexicographer and noted literary light, was not exaggerating much when he remarked, "No man will be a sailor who has contrivance enough to get himself into a jail; for being in a ship is being in a jail with the chance of being drowned. A man in a jail has more room, better food and commonly better company."[16]

Commissioned officers realized that there was a limit to what seamen would endure before they mutinied, and so, since the men could not seek sexual gratification on shore, when a ship came into harbor, prostitutes were allowed to stay with the seamen on board. (It was also feared that there would be an increase in cases of homosexuality if the men did not have some opportunities for concourse with women.)

Complaints about lack of leave go back to the Dutch wars in the seventeenth century. In a petition to Oliver Cromwell in 1654, seamen protested the order that denied them leave and kept them "in thraldom and bondage."[17] The situation did not improve in the eighteenth century. Following the great mutiny at Spithead in 1797, lack of leave was the only major grievance of the mutineers that was not remedied. It was not until the 1830s, by which time men were no longer pressed and living conditions on board were greatly improved, that most captains granted leave on a regular basis. (There were no Admiralty regulations or guidelines regarding shore leave; it was entirely the responsibility of each vessel's commander to decide how much, if any, leave to give.)

A few humane officers, who had treated their crews decently, dared to give leave, and their men, grateful for the indulgence, proved they could be trusted. Just prior to the 1797 Spithead mutiny, Admiral Charles Vinicombe Penrose let his men go ashore in rotation, a few at a time, and only two deserted. Captain Anselm John Griffiths lost only eleven out of three hundred when he gave his crew leave in 1811.[18] These were exceptional cases, however. Most commissioned officers were part of the upper middle class or of the gentry, and in the sharply delineated class system of their time they looked upon their seamen, who were part of the underclass, as a separate, inferior species who could be controlled only by harsh discipline.

The Seaman's Hard Lot

To understand the horrors endured by the seamen's prostitutes, it is necessary to know how brutalized the seamen themselves were.

Life on land was hard for a man of the poorer classes, but it was seldom as bad as life on the lower deck of a naval vessel. Naval punishment was often draconian; a seaman could be flogged for the most minor offense. Drinking water was foul, and the men's diet was monotonous as well as unhealthy, consisting primarily of heavily salted meat, dried peas, sea biscuits, and hard cheese. The seamen slept, ate, and spent what leisure time they had on the badly ventilated lower gun deck, which reeked of bilge water, human waste, and sweat.

The great killer of naval seamen was neither shipwreck nor battle but disease. Between 1792 and 1815, during which time Britain was, except for one year, continuously at war, half of all naval deaths were from disease. Although the number of deaths gradually decreased over the years as medical treatment, diet, and sanitation improved, the death rate continued to be dreadfully high. Sir Gilbert Blane, the great naval physician, reported that in 1815 the navy's mortality rate from disease was 1 in 30.25, although most of the seamen were in the prime of life, between the ages of twenty and forty. National mortality for that age group was only 1 in 80.[19]

Scurvy, caused by a lack of vitamin C, was a ghastly disease that rotted the gums so that the teeth fell out, and a major killer of seamen whose diet was almost totally lacking in fresh fruits and vegetables and fresh meat. It was not until 1795 that a daily issue of lemon or lime juice was required in all ships; the use of *limey* as a nickname for British sailors came from this requirement.

Typhus, spread by body lice and rats, often reached epidemic proportions in the channel fleet, where infected recruits were sent on board still wearing their lice-ridden clothing. Influenza, consumption (tuberculosis), dysentery, and smallpox also took a heavy toll.[20] The seamen's greatest fear, however, and rightly so, was that they would be sent to the West Indies, where yellow fever raged. It was not unusual for a ship with a complement of several hundred to lose all but a handful of her men to that disease.[21]

Although it was not known that tropical diseases such as yellow fever and malaria were carried by mosquitoes, officers were aware that men sent on shore were especially vulnerable to these maladies, especially if they remained into the evening, when mosquitoes are most active. This knowledge provided another reason for keeping the men on board, anchoring far from shore, and, in turn, sending crowds of women into the ships.

A man tempted to desert was seldom deterred by thoughts of future pay. Wages remained the same from 1653 until 1797, although the economy had greatly inflated during those 144 years.[22] Seamen's wages were raised following the 1797 mutinies at Spithead and the Nore, but this does not mean that they were paid on time. The navy was continuously short of cash, and the men waited months, even years, for their pay. In 1811 Lord Thomas Cochrane begged Parliament to see that seamen were paid on a regular basis. He presented a list of ships in the East Indies whose crews had not been paid for eleven, fourteen, and even fifteen years, but his fellow parliamentarians were unmoved. The response to Cochrane's plea was that the situation "was much to be regretted, but it was often unavoidable." The subject was dropped.[23]

On top of all this was the fact that a large percentage of naval crews had been forced on board in the first place—grabbed by press gangs with no chance to arrange matters at home before they were taken away. In wartime—which in the Georgian era was most of the time—ships were often so short of men that it was necessary to call for "a hot press" in which gangs were sent out to grab any man they could catch who could not prove himself a member of the gentry. Every coastal town in England had its terrible stories, only slightly exaggerated in the telling, of gangs who broke into houses and pulled men from their beds, or of bridegrooms captured at the altar and carried off to sea.

George Cruikshank, "Tars Carousing," a view of the lower deck in port. From T. Dibdin, ed., *Songs of the Late Charles Dibdin*, 3d ed. (London: Henry G. Bohn, 1864), frontispiece. BOSTON ATHENAEUM

Press gangs also waylaid merchant vessels as they headed home and took off their most experienced seamen. Sometimes they removed the entire crew, putting their own men on board to bring the vessel in. It was heartbreaking for sailors to be impressed just when they were returning home from a long voyage.

For a time, convicted smugglers who could not pay a fine were offered a choice of jail or the navy, but so many agreed with Dr. Johnson and chose jail that the law was changed so that all convicted smugglers were sent into the navy.[24]

The most disaffected of all the seamen were the foreigners—they made up an average of around 12 percent of crews during the Napoleonic Wars—especially those taken on board from captured enemy ships.[25] Nor were the black slaves, sent into the navy by their masters, stirred by patriotic fervor. Slaves served as seamen at least until 1772, when slavery was effectively abolished in Great Britain; and in West Indian ports, until its abolition there in 1833, slaves were brought on board to work ships whose crews had been decimated by disease.[26]

Officers were well aware of the disaffection of large numbers of their men, but there was little they could, or would, do to compensate for the men's hard life and lack of freedom, except to provide them with great quantities of liquor—there was an allowance of a gallon of beer and a half-pint of rum per man per day—and the company of women when ships were in port.[27] Admiral Charles Vinicombe Penrose, writing in 1824, summed up the officers' attitude about having prostitutes on board: "Allowing women of bad character [on board] is an ancient custom, always forbidden, either by general or particular instruction, but always allowed...as a necessary or rather unavoidable evil."[28]

Admiralty Regulations

A Tudor disciplinary code predating 1553 included the order, "No woman to lie a shippe borde all nyght."[29] The fact that it was necessary to issue this regulation indicates that it was commonplace for women to spend the night on board even at that early date. By the eighteenth century the tradition of allowing huge numbers of prostitutes to frequent naval ships was firmly established.

In the first printed *Regulations and Instructions Relating to His Majesty's Service at Sea*, issued in 1731, no mention was made of women coming on board in port, although commanding officers were ordered "not to carry any woman to sea...without orders from the Admiralty."[30] By the 1750s, however, the following peevish instructions had been appended under "Additional Regulations": "That no woman be ever permitted to be on board but such as are really the wives of the men they come to, and the ship not to be too much pestered even with them."[31] These instructions were in a section entitled "Rules for Preserving Cleanliness," in which officers were also ordered to see that "the men keep themselves as clean in every respect as possible"—a vague directive if ever there was one—and were instructed "to prevent peoples' easing themselves in the hold or throwing anything there that may occasion nastiness."[32] Moral cleanliness was not distinguished from physical cleanliness. (At that period the euphemism *unclean acts* was often substituted for the taboo words *buggery* and *sodomy*.)

The instruction to admit only wives of seamen was seldom followed, and a captain who tried to enforce it was made fun of by his fellow officers. Sir William Henry Dillon noted in his memoirs that Captain James Gambier, "a strictly devout, religious man bordering upon the Methodist principle," upon taking command of the *Defence* in 1793 ordered that all women coming on board must show wedding certificates. "Those that had any produced them," Dillon reported, "and those that had not, contrived to manufacture a few. This measure created a very unpleasant feeling amongst the tars."[33]

Equally bad feelings resulted from the following orders issued by Captain Richard G. Keats in H.M.S. *Superb* in 1803:

> In port, women will be permitted to come on board, but this indulgence is to be granted (as indeed are all others) in proportion to the merits of the men who require them, and upon their being accountable for the conduct of the women with them.
>
> The commanding officer in port will therefore permit such men to have women on board as he may choose: and he will direct the master-at-arms to keep a list agreeable to the following form; which he will carry to the commanding officer every morning for his inspection.[34]

The following questions were to be answered: "Women's names? With whom? Married or single? When received on board? Conduct?"

It seems highly unlikely that the master-at-arms was capable of keeping a detailed daily list of the individual women. Amid the hubbub of the crowded ship, he was lucky if he could prevent the women from smuggling liquor on board and could keep brawling to a minimum.

In 1829 the puritanical Lieutenant Robert Wauchope was appointed flag captain to Sir Patrick Campbell. Wauchope insisted that he would accept the appointment only if prostitutes were kept out of the ship. Campbell could not allow his junior to bargain over his promotion, and so he sent the impertinent young officer to appear before the Admiralty. The First Sea Lord, Admiral Thomas Hardy—who had been the boon companion of Horatio Nelson—conducted the interview. Here is a compressed version:

Hardy: I understand you object to women going on board.
Wauchope: I object to prostitutes going on board.
Hardy: You go contrary to the wishes of the Admiralty and will therefore give up your commission.
Wauchope: No. If the Admiralty choose to *take* my commission on this account, they may. I will not give it up.
Hardy: As one of the Lords of Admiralty, I consider it right that women should be admitted into ships; when I was at sea, I always admitted them....
Wauchope: Sir Thomas, it is written that *whoremongers shall not enter heaven.* Many officers hold the same opinion about admitting women aboard as I do.
Hardy: I am sorry to hear it sir.... You have given up your commission.[35]

Apparently Wauchope finally agreed to give up his stand on the issue, for he received his commission, and eventually he himself rose to the rank of admiral.

The Hard Case of Seamen's Wives

Seamen's wives led a hard life. Men caught by a press gang had no time to arrange for the maintenance of their families while they were at sea. Often an impressed man simply disappeared from his wife's life; she might not hear from him for years, even if he survived the rigors of the navy. Samuel Pepys described in his diary on 1 July 1666 the anguish of a group of women he saw at the Tower of London, where newly impressed men were collected and carried off to the navy:

> To the Tower, about the business of the pressed men. But, Lord, how some poor women did cry; and in my life I never did see such natural expression of passion as I did here in some women's bewailing themselves, and running to every parcel of men that was brought, one after another to look for their husbands, and wept over every vessel that went off, thinking they might be there and looking after the ship as far as ever they could by moonlight, that it grieved me to the heart to hear them.[36]

When a seaman's ship returned to England, his wife seldom knew in advance when or where his vessel would arrive. When she did learn that her husband's ship was in, if she was living far from his place of arrival she probably had to get there on foot, since not many wives could afford to pay for a seat on a stagecoach or coastal vessel. It was a common sight on the lonely roads of Devon and Cornwall, where so many seamen came from, to see a group of seamen's wives and their ragged children stumbling along toward Plymouth or distant Portsmouth. West-country wives of seamen whose ships anchored at the Nore (at the mouth of the Thames) or the Downs (near the point where the North Sea meets the English Channel) found it even more difficult to get to their husbands. The prostitutes were usually well settled on the lower deck by the time the seamen's families reached the ship. When a seaman's wife finally got on board, there was nowhere she could be alone with her husband. She, and her children if she brought them along, had no choice but to join the raucous crowd on the lower deck.

But however unpleasant it was on board, it was important for a seaman's wife to be present when at long last the men were paid. Unless she was there, she was unlikely to get any of her husband's wages; the system of sending allotments to seamen's families was inefficient at best. When payday at last arrived, the crew lined up on deck, each man holding his wide-brimmed, tarred black hat. Each man's wages, in cash, were placed in his hat and the amount was chalked on the brim. The money was quickly spent. The purser had to be paid for the tobacco and slops (ready-made clothing) a seaman had purchased on credit from the slop chest during the voyage. A man's accounts with the bumboat men and women also had to be paid. And if a man's wife had not been staying on board, he probably owed money to a prostitute.[37]

There was very little possibility that a seaman could save any of his wages for his and his family's future. Except for rare instances when he received a sizable amount of prize money—his share of the proceeds from the sale of a vessel and her cargo that had been captured by his ship—he lived hand to mouth.[38]

On the day before a ship sailed, amid the general confusion of last-minute preparations for departure, the women on board—with the exception of those few who were going to sea—bid farewell to their men, whom they might never see again. A late-eighteenth-century ballad relates:

> *Our ship she is all rigg'd and ready for sea, boys;*
>   *The girls that's on board they begin to look blue;*
> *The boats are alongside to take them on shore, boys;*
>   *Says one to the other, "Girls, what shall we do?"*[39]

In ships sailing from the Nore or the Downs, the women often were not sent on shore until the vessel made her last call at an English port in the Channel before heading out to sea. The women then had to get home from that port as best they could. Some of the wives in chaplain Teonge's ship in 1675 remained on board when she sailed from the Downs. They were supposed to disembark at Deal but were not sent ashore until Dover. They left in the ship's pinnace at six in the morning, and according to Teonge, their departure was honored "with three cheers, seven guns, and our trumpets sounding."[40] Teonge was wrong about the salute; whomever it was for, it was certainly not for the women.

Starving Wives at Home

Wives of seamen struggled to keep themselves and their children from starvation while their husbands were at sea. Even if a wife had been on board on payday to get her share of her husband's wages, the money did not last long. The government attempted to play down the plight of penniless seamen's wives, but its efforts to repress their sad stories were not very effective.

Poor seamen's wives were a popular subject of street ballads. Ballads, quickly composed to convey the scandals and important events of the day, were the primary source of news for the lower classes. The ballad "The Sea Martyrs," from around 1690, for example, revealed the case of the men of H.M.S. *Suffolk* who were executed as mutineers for their protests over lack of pay. One verse related:

> *Their poor wives with care languished,*
> *Their children cried for want of bread.*
> *Their debts encreast, and none would more*
> *Lend them, or let them run o' th' score.*[41]

In other words, the women's creditors refused to extend their credit. The government was so disturbed by the subversive message of "The Sea Martyrs" that a balladeer could be arrested and flogged for singing it.

From 1758 onward, legally a seaman could have an allotment of a few pence a day sent to his wife, but the system was so complicated—perhaps intentionally so—that very few seamen knew how to make the initial arrangements. In 1759, in seventy-two ships that were paid off at Plymouth, only 3 percent of the men made remittances to their families.[42] It was not until 1858, at the very end of the period we are dealing with, that a workable allotment system was established.

Some officers helped their men send money home. Admiral Edward Boscawen always tried to make arrangements through private channels to enable his men to send some of their wages to their wives. In a letter from Portsmouth to his own wife, dated 26 April 1756, he wrote, "Our men have been paid, and what is very extra-ordinary, have paid into my hands 563 pounds, 9 shillings to send to their wives all over Britain."[43] On the whole, however, officers gave little attention to the general welfare of their men, let alone the men's wives.

Seamen's wives who were left behind in Portsmouth or Plymouth found it almost impossible to find work. Except for the all-male naval yards, there was little industry in either town, and very few seamen's wives had the necessary references to be hired into domestic service, where the greatest percentage of jobs for females were to be found. They were forced to seek public charity.

Both towns were inundated with indigent seamen's wives and children. The Guardians of the Poor, the officials in charge of public charity, were continuously struggling to keep this multitude from draining the towns' relief funds. The Guardians' main solution to the problem was to pack the women off to their home parishes (their birthplace or last place of residence). From 1662, when the law known as the Act of Settlement and Removal was passed, paupers (people living on public charity) who were non-residents were disposed of in this way.[44]

Paupers, including seamen's wives awaiting transportation to their home parishes, were sent to the workhouse. Workhouses, paid for out of local taxes, were always underfunded and usually mismanaged. Almost without exception they were full of misery, disease, and death. Able-bodied inmates were put to work at menial jobs such as picking oakum (strands of hemp used to caulk ship's planking) or plaiting straw for sailor's hats, the proceeds of which went to the institution. But there were numbers of inmates who were unable to work. These unfortunates, known as the "impotent poor," included infants, the aged, the blind, the insane, and the diseased (both chronic invalids and those with contagious diseases). Prostitutes disabled from sexually transmitted diseases often were sent to a workhouse.

All the inmates both sick and well were housed together, and, not surprisingly, the death rate was high, especially among infants. A committee appointed by the House of Commons in 1767 to examine the conditions in workhouses throughout England reported that between 1763 and 1765, of all the infants born in these institutions or who were received when under twelve months old, only seven in a hundred survived their first year.[45] Some seamen's wives became prostitutes rather than expose their children to the dangers of a workhouse.

The first workhouse in Portsmouth was founded in 1729, and by 1764 there was also a workhouse in the adjoining residential community of Portsea. In 1801 there were at least three in the Portsmouth area.[46] All of them were crowded with seamen's wives, most of them awaiting transportation to their home parishes.

Plymouth taxpayers were also burdened with the expense of sending home scores of destitute seamen's families. There were so many of these families in Plymouth in 1758 that special legislation had to be initiated by the county to raise the funds necessary to send all of them to their home parishes.[47]

The first workhouse in Plymouth, established in 1708, took over from the Hospital of Poor's Portion, a church-run almshouse founded in 1615.[48] It had a terrible reputation for its harsh rules and crowded, unsanitary conditions. In 1727 a report of the Guardians of the Workhouse, in order to show that acceptable discipline was maintained, recorded the whipping of a woman and her daughter "for not performing the task set them."[49] Many of the buildings of the Poor's Portion workhouse, constructed in 1630, continued to house inmates until 1851, when they were finally torn down, "being in a loathsome condition."[50]

Seamen's wives who tried to avoid the workhouse by begging could be arrested, jailed, and then sent to their home parishes under the vagrancy laws rather than the poor laws. Beginning in 1597 vagrants were to be whipped and imprisoned before being sent home. After 1750 female vagrants were seldom whipped, and by the late eighteenth century most vagrants were simply shipped off without being punished first.[51]

A seaman's wife who turned to begging not only risked arrest, she also had to compete with the bands of skilled beggars, including disabled seamen and their women, who roamed throughout England. (Even those disabled seamen who received a pension could not survive on it alone.) In 1787 the *Leeds Intelligencer* reported the presence of such a band in that inland town:

> Last week five or six sailors, or pretended sailors, maimed or without a leg or an arm, or both, who wander through the Kingdom with the model of a ship, living on continual vagrancy…were lodged in the House of Correction at Wakefield, in order to be sent to their several homes. Several women belonging to them disperse themselves in the daytime, begging, telling fortunes, etc. in different parts; the whole gang usually assemble together at nights…in obscure lodging houses, meeting with other idle and dangerous persons.[52]

A number of ballads told of the plight of disabled seamen and their wives, not always sympathetically. An example is the comic ballad "Oh! Cruel," in which a disabled seaman's wife describes how she and her husband are forced to beg for a living:

> *Oh! cruel was th' engagement in which my true love fought,*
> *   And cruel was the cannon ball that knock'd his right eye out;*
> *He us'd to leer and ogle me with peepers full of fun,*
> *   But now he looks askew at me, because he has but one.*

> *Oh! cruel was the splinter to break my deary's leg,*
> *   Now he's obliged to fiddle, and I'm obliged to beg;*
> *A vagabonding vagrant, and a rantipoling [whoring] wife,*
> *   We fiddle, limp, and scrape it, thro' the ups and downs of life.*[53]

Once a seaman's wife arrived back in her home community, unless she had relatives to care for her or could find a job, she still was faced with the choice of prostitution, begging, or public charity. Even those wives who found factory work often lapsed into prostitution rather than continue to work ten- and twelve-hour days, six days a week for inadequate pay.

When a wife heard that her husband's ship had again returned to an English port, the process of going to his ship and then being sent home as a pauper started all over again.

Wives Turned Prostitute (and Vice Versa)

A popular subject of eighteenth-century prints and drawings was the seaman's prim young wife. The stereotype, still accepted today, was that a seaman's wife was good, patient, and faithful while the seaman's whore was bad, drunken, and dishonest. Actually, the line between wife and prostitute was thin; seamen's wives often turned to prostitution while their husbands were at sea.

Contemporary ballads did not always make this faulty contrast between good wife and bad whore. A ballad of the late seventeenth century, "The Seamen's Wives' Vindication," purports to refute the accusation that seamen's wives are drunken and promiscuous. Actually, it reinforces the view of the wives as carousing prostitutes. The following verses are representative of the ballad's rather muddled lyrics:

> Here you have newly reported that we are girls of the game,
>   Who do delight to be courted. Are you not highly to blame,
> Saying we often are merry, punch is the liquor we praise,
>   Though we are known to be weary of these our sorrowing days?
>
> How could you say there were many wives that did drink, rant,
>   and sing,
> When I protest there's not any of us that practice this thing?
>   Are we not forced to borrow, being left here without clink?
> 'Tis in a cup of cold sorrow if we so often do drink.[54]

While many seamen's wives became seamen's prostitutes, the reverse was also true. When a seaman came ashore at the end of his vessel's commission, it was not unusual for him to get married to a friendly prostitute. Up to 1754, when the Marriage Act forbidding quick marriages was passed, he could do this on a sudden impulse at one of the special chapels in London, most of them in the neighborhood of the Fleet Prison, where there was no waiting period.[55] (In regular churches banns had to be read for three consecutive weeks before a wedding could take place.) In 1753 the Reverend Alexander Keith, who ran a quick-marriage chapel in Mayfair, wrote down the following incident:

> I was at a public-house at Radcliffe, which was then full of sailors and their girls; there was fiddling, piping, jigging, and eating; at length one of the tars starts up and says, "D——m ye, Jack, I'll be married just now; I will have my partner, and...." The joke took, and in less than two hours ten couple[s] set out for the Fleet. I staid [until] their return. They returned in coaches; five women in each coach; the tars some running before, others riding on the coach box; and others behind. The Cavalcade being over, the couples went up into an upper room, where they concluded the evening with great jollity. The next time I went that way, I called on my landlord and asked him concerning this marriage adventure; he first stared at me, but recollecting, he said those things were so frequent, that he hardly took any notice of them, for, added he, it is a common thing, when a fleet comes in, to have two or three hundred marriages in a week's time among the sailors.[56]

SEAMEN'S PROSTITUTES ON LAND

Legal Status

Although the prostitutes of Portsmouth and Plymouth made up a considerable part of the population of those towns, they formed no cohesive group and had no political power and next to no legal rights. For that matter, few women, regardless of their social station, controlled their own lives, but respectable women were protected by their status within society. Prostitutes were particularly powerless; not only were they female and part of the great majority of the illiterate, unskilled underclass, but they lived outside the bounds of acceptable cultural standards. Prostitutes were open to ridicule and degradation and to both physical and emotional abuse that would not have been countenanced if directed toward respectable women.

Throughout the eighteenth and nineteenth centuries prostitution was rife in the towns and cities of England. As the country shifted from an agricultural society to a largely industrial one, great segments of the population moved from rural areas to urban centers. Many young women were uprooted from the country parishes where they had been part of a tightly knit, relatively stable community and thrown into the unfamiliar, hostile environment of city slums. These were times when most women were socially as well as financially dependent on their male family ties. A woman's social status was related to the status of the male head of her household. A young working-class woman without a man to maintain her—father, husband, or brother—was an outcast. She had neither social nor economic stability.

Prostitution was never in itself against the law, with the exception of one two-year period from 1822 to 1824. So long as a prostitute was not unruly, she was allowed to ply her trade without official interference. There were, however, many attempts to legislate against prostitution. In 1770 Sir John Fielding, the eminent London magistrate who, with his brother Henry, the novelist and judge, organized the first London police force, attempted to get a law passed under which prostitutes could be arrested under the vagrancy laws (together with ballad singers, who also loitered on the public thoroughfares); but he was unsuccessful.[57]

Under the Vagrancy Act of 1822 a prostitute could be arrested as "an idle and disorderly person" simply for soliciting. The law specified, "All common prostitutes or night-walkers wandering in public streets or highways and not giving a satisfactory account of themselves are to be deemed idle and disorderly persons, and as such liable to a month's imprisonment."[58] In 1824 another Vagrancy Act was passed that returned to the earlier practice of arresting only those "common prostitutes" who behaved in public "in a riotous or indecent manner."[59] (The term *common prostitute* denoted a woman whose customers shared her "in common," as distinguished from a mistress, who was supported by one man.)

For centuries prostitution, both in naval ships and in naval ports, was intentionally ignored by the Admiralty. It was not until the late 1850s, by which time prostitutes seldom came into naval ships, that the Admiralty began to take an active role in the control of prostitution in naval ports. At that time both the navy and the army became concerned over the epidemic of venereal disease among their men. They did not, however, try to control the disease by focusing on soldiers and sailors; they focused on the single women living in the areas around army bases and naval stations. In the 1860s a series of laws were passed—called the Contagious Diseases Acts (Women), a euphemism for venereal diseases acts— that closely involved the navy and the army. In designated districts, including Portsmouth and Plymouth, plainclothes police were sent out to identify prostitutes and to place their names on an official list. Any lower-class young single woman living alone was liable to be listed as a prostitute with no way to disprove this designation. Once a woman was listed, she was forced to be examined every few weeks for sexually transmitted disease, and if found to be infected, she was sent into a hospital lock ward (a facility specifically for the treatment of venereal disease) for a period of up to nine months. The laws were repealed in 1866, after years of agitation by social reformers, who protested that the acts were prejudicial to women, as indeed they were.[60]

Numbers

Before the 1850s, when the navy began to take an interest in the prostitutes of Portsmouth and Plymouth, the regulation of prostitution rested solely with local authorities, who ignored the existence of these women as much as possible and took no action against them unless they were disorderly. There are therefore almost no data on the prostitutes of these naval ports. Their numbers, their average age, and their way of life on shore can only be inferred from a few random records, the passing impressions of a few individuals, and the highly colored propaganda of social reformers.

The reformers were more interested in gaining public support for their mission "to rescue fallen women" than in collecting accurate data on prostitution. In 1824, for example, a naval surgeon's pamphlet against allowing women in naval vessels estimated that there were twenty thousand prostitutes in Portsmouth. The 1821 census puts the combined population of Portsmouth, Portsea, and Gosport at less than sixty thousand; according to the surgeon's estimate, then, one in three people in the area would have been a prostitute.[61] The figure is wildly exaggerated.

Census data, from the first census in 1801 onward, do show a preponderance of females in both Portsmouth and Plymouth, even though the main industry in each town was the dockyards, which hired at most a handful of women. In the census of 1821, for example, there were 4,798 more females than males in the combined population of Portsmouth and Portsea, even though wives of seamen and soldiers awaiting transportation to their home parishes were not counted.[62]

There is no record of there ever being a shortage of women to fill naval ships in Portsmouth and Plymouth, even when a whole fleet arrived. There are a number of mentions of over four hundred women coming into a single vessel, and the seaman Samuel Stokes noted in his memoirs that on one payday in 1809 the ninety-eight-gun *Dreadnought,* with a complement of eight hundred men, had on board "thirteen women more than the number of our ship's company and not fifty of them married women."[63] It is apparent that more than one thousand prostitutes were always available.

Whatever the total number of prostitutes in naval ports may have been, it is unlikely that so many of them have ever been gathered together in one enclosed space at any time in history as were regularly assembled on the lower decks of vessels of the Royal Navy in the eighteenth and early nineteenth centuries.

The Prostitutes' Way of Life

The prostitutes who lived in naval ships in port were at the very bottom of the social and economic ladder; only the most desperate woman would enter the nightmare world of the lower deck to sell her services to any man who chose her. Her partner might be anyone from a naive young boy to an "incorrigible rogue."

At the beginning of a war, when the navy needed to raise large numbers of men in a hurry, it took in convicted rogues and vagabonds from jail. When war with France started up in 1744, an act of Parliament was passed that ordered that "any rogue or vagabond of the male sex over twelve years of age, after punishment, [was] to be employed by His Majesty's service by sea or by land." And again in 1756, at the beginning of the Seven Years' War, an order was sent out "to impress loose and disorderly persons."[64]

In 1795 the shortage of men was so severe that the Quota Acts were passed, which required magistrates in every county in England to provide, within a period of three weeks, a specified quota of men for the navy based on the population of the county. To fulfill these quotas, communities cleared their jails.[65] Admiral Cuthbert Collingwood wrote to his sister in 1797 that "the refuse of the gallows and the parings of a gaol…make the majority of most ships' companies in such a war as this."[66]

There was a good chance that a prostitute's partner was suffering from a sexually transmitted disease. Until 1795 a seaman had to pay the ship's surgeon fifteen shillings—most of a month's wages—in order to receive treatment for a venereal disease. Many, therefore, avoided treatment.[67] After 1795 treatment was free, but there were no regulations to ensure regular physical examinations of seamen. In any event, the various stages of the diseases, especially syphilis, were not well understood. In fact, until 1793 syphilis and gonorrhea were generally thought to be the same disease. Treatment was not very effective. The primary remedy was mercury, applied as an ointment or ingested in the form of quicksilver as a purge—dangerous in itself.[68]

A prostitute, especially a ship's prostitute, was unable to protect herself from either venereal disease or pregnancy. Some women were made sterile by gonorrhea, but for most of them, pregnancy, like infection, was a constant specter. In the 1820s and 1830s a few middle-class women used douches and vaginal sponges, with alum, bicarbonate of soda, or vinegar. These might have afforded slight protection if used immediately after coitus, but they were impossible for prostitutes to use on board ship.[69] Although condoms had been used in England by upper-class men for both prophylaxis and contraception since the seventeenth century, in the eighteenth and nineteenth centuries they were still expensive and considered effete. They were made of lamb's gut, cleaned and rubbed with bran and almond oil, and, when put on, secured with ribbons tied around the scrotum.[70] It is impossible to imagine a tough old tar using one, even if he knew such a thing existed.

An infected ship's prostitute found it difficult to get medical treatment. Private physicians were much too expensive, and clinics and hospitals often refused to admit women suffering from venereal disease, especially known prostitutes. In the latter part of the eighteenth century some cities set up lock wards for women, but there was none in Portsmouth until an Admiralty-sponsored one was opened in 1858. In Plymouth the first such facility, also sponsored by the Admiralty, was opened in 1863.[71] Both were started after the period we are dealing with. Earlier, if a prostitute was so sick that she could not work, she usually ended up in the public workhouse as one of the unemployable "impotent poor," where she received little or no medical treatment.

It was taken for granted by most people that sexually transmitted diseases represented the wages of sin and that the sufferers deserved what they got. Even many doctors believed that sexually transmitted diseases were caused by excessive sexual activity. Symptoms of gonorrhea in a woman were not considered to be serious and were often ignored. When treatment was provided, it was largely ineffectual and sometimes harmful, consisting of warm baths, salves, and medicines that included such dangerous ingredients as sugar of lead and vitriol.[72]

In addition to sexually transmitted diseases, ship's prostitutes were victims of the other contagious diseases that afflicted naval crews. And unsanitary living conditions, on land as well as on board, combined with a bad diet and quantities of cheap gin, increased their vulnerability.

Ship's prostitutes worked independently. They earned too little to be sponsored by the madams who ran bawdyhouses. They rented rooms in cheap lodging houses and also shared the quarters of poor families who welcomed even the small rent a ship's prostitute could afford. Often several prostitutes shared a small room.[73] In Portsmouth many of the ship's prostitutes lived in dilapidated buildings along the congested lanes flanking High Street, or on the Point, the spit of land crisscrossed by streets full of low sailors' taverns. Others lived in poor sections of Portsea, earlier called the Common, or across the water in Gosport.[74] In Plymouth many prostitutes lived in rented rooms in the district of sailors' taverns surrounding Castle Street near Plymouth Quay, known to seamen as Castle Rag or Damnation Alley.[75] Both the Portsmouth and the Plymouth slums incubated all the ills that go with lack of sewers, tainted water, and crowded, airless living quarters.

While some ship's prostitutes grew up in the local slums, a number came to town from the surrounding countryside, especially in times of crop failure or general economic depression. Admiral Hawker reported in the 1820s that officials in a country parish bordering on Hampshire regularly sent "young women who were likely to become burdensome...to Portsmouth, from whence they never returned."[76] In 1871 a Plymouth magistrate found that four out of five of the registered prostitutes in greater Plymouth were from the neighboring rural areas of Cornwall, and one can assume that this was the pattern earlier in the century as well.[77]

It appears likely that a large number of ship's prostitutes were startlingly young. Samuel Leech, a seaman in the Anglo-American War of 1812, noted that "many of the lost unfortunate creatures" brought into his ship "were in the springtime of life," and in that same period the seaman William Robinson referred to the prostitutes in his ship as "poor young creatures."[78] In both London and Edinburgh, where, unlike Portsmouth and Plymouth, a good deal of information about prostitutes was gathered, many prostitutes were little more than adolescents. In the 1750s the magistrate John Fielding said that most of the inmates of London brothels were under eighteen and many no older than twelve.[79] A London relief organization reported in 1813, "The number of abandoned children from the age of twelve to fourteen years living in a state of prostitution who are brought daily before the magistrates for petty crimes, are increased to an alarming degree within these few years."[80] And William Tait, house surgeon at the lock hospital in Edinburgh, found that between 1835 and 1839, of the one thousand prostitutes admitted, half were between the ages of fifteen and twenty, forty-two were under fifteen, and one was nine.[81]

At a time when factories hired children of six or seven to work a ten- or twelve-hour day, and warships carried midshipmen of ten or eleven as well as a number of adolescent boys in the crew, it is not surprising to find that officers and seamen alike accepted the fact that very young prostitutes came on board. It was not until 1861 that legislation was passed against the use of girls under twelve for immoral purposes. The age of consent (to sexual congress) for females was twelve throughout the period we are dealing with. In 1871 it was raised to thirteen, not a great step forward, and in 1885, to sixteen.[82]

The prostitutes of Portsmouth and Plymouth were a popular subject of eighteenth- and nineteenth-century prints and watercolors by such well-known artists as George Cruikshank and Thomas Rowlandson. Almost all of these illustrations present the popular stereotype of the prostitute: large, muscular, buxom women in their thirties or forties, with coarse features and leering expressions. These caricatures bear little resemblance to the undersized, often sickly teenagers who actually served the seamen.

The same stereotype is found in written portrayals of prostitutes. Dr. George Pinckard's description of "Portsmouth Polls," in 1795, is typical of the genre:

> To form to yourself an idea of these tender, languishing nymphs, these lovely, fighting ornaments of the fair sex, imagine a something of more than Amazonian stature, having a crimson countenance, emblazoned with all the effrontery of Cyprian confidence and broad Bacchanalian folly; give to her bold countenance the warlike features of two wounded cheeks, a tumid nose, scarred and battered brows, and a pair of blackened eyes, with balls of red; then add to her sides a pair of brawny arms, fit to encounter a Colossus, and set her upon two ankles like the fixed supporters of a gate. Afterwards, by way of apparel, put upon her a loose flying cap, a man's black hat, a torn neckerchief, stone rings on her fingers, and a dirty white, or tawdry flowered gown, with short apron, and a pink petticoat; and thus will you have something very like the figure of a "Portsmouth Poll."[83]

A very different picture is presented in the only actual firsthand report I have found about an individual ship's prostitute. It comes from the journal of Robert Mercer Wilson, a seaman in H.M.S. *Unité* from 1805 to 1809:

> A good-looking young woman was taken in [the vessel] one day by a messmate of mine. When he brought her below, I observed that in spite of her trying to be cheerful, she was sad and many a sigh escaped her.... My thoughtless messmates...were more mindful of pleasure than noticing whether their girls were glad or sad.... For my part I observed her sighs, and from her discourse I found her to be a woman of some learning....
>
> I leave my readers to guess how I was surprised and amazed when I perceived her to be big with child. "Good God!" said I to myself, "well might she sigh and look sad." What had hindered myself and my messmates from observing it before was she had so artfully concealed it...that it was impossible to perceive it till she took off her cloak....
>
> In spite of my remonstrances with my messmate not to have any connections with her, my offering to take her off his hands, which made him think I was anxious to possess her charms, made him the more determined to satisfy his ———.
>
> Poor girl! It was a dear bought pleasure for her, for next morning she was seized with convulsions severe, which indicated the quick birth of the infant in her womb. When her situation was made known, our First and Second Lieutenants (to their honour be it said) gave her a guinea each; I contributed a small matter, but not half so much as I could wish, and she went on shore.
>
> The next day a letter came from her (though not written by her) to this effect; "that she [had] scarcely arrived on shore before she was delivered of a fine boy, in a promising state." She desired her compliments to me, and I wrote her an answer back. I must confess, only for the esteem I bore for the girl I loved, my heart might have been smitten with the charms of that unfortunate fair one, so prepossessed was I in her favour. To conclude, I had afterwards the pleasure to hear that all went well with her, and she expected soon to join her friends, who had received her into their good graces.[84]

THE REFORM MOVEMENT AND THE PROSTITUTES

Private Efforts

Beginning around 1750 a long period of social reform began. It started in London and soon spread throughout Great Britain. Close to a hundred organizations and societies, financed totally by private funds, were formed to address every imaginable social evil from the slave trade and the plight of "climbing boys" (chimney sweeps) to the salvation of prostitutes.

The spirit of reform even penetrated the upper echelons of the navy, a bastion of conservatism. A number of naval officers became actively involved in seeking reform in the navy itself. Among the noted admirals who were active in the reform movement was Richard Kempenfelt, who, when his flagship the *Royal George* sank in 1782, had on board, in addition to four hundred prostitutes, four hundred Bibles—the first allotment of Bibles donated for the uplift of seamen by the Naval and Military Bible Society.[85] (Admiral Kempenfelt, the prostitutes, and the Bibles were lost.) Another Evangelical admiral, whom we have already mentioned, was Lord (James) Gambier, known throughout the navy as Preaching Jemmy. Still others were Baron de Saumarez (James Saumarez), Viscount Exmouth (Edward Pellew), and Lord Barham (Charles Middleton), first lord of the Admiralty.

How effective the reformers were, both inside and outside the navy, in their campaign against prostitution is open to question. They focused on moral uplift rather than on improving the economic conditions that engendered prostitution; their aim was to rid the nation of vice, not to alter the economic status quo or the class system. These middle-class reformers were strongly opposed to radical social thought such as that of Tom Paine and to political action by the poor themselves. The reformers talked a great deal about the importance of "fidelity" among the lower classes, by which they meant fidelity to the standards set by the upper classes. They also firmly believed that immorality promoted social dissolution.

We tend to think that sentimentality and condescension were the special province of the Victorians, but eighteenth- and early-nineteenth-century reformers were also restricted by narrow, class-bound, pious, and sentimental attitudes. They, like the Victorians who followed them, were diligent in their efforts to rescue the "deserving poor" and "repentant prostitutes"; the undeserving and the unrepentant could go hang—and often did, in a period when even petty theft was a capital offense.

A sampling of the names of institutions formed "to rescue" indigent young girls and prostitutes reveals the bias of the reformers: the Asylum for Poor, Friendless, Deserted Girls under Twelve Years of Age (founded 1758); the Lock Asylum for the Reception of Penitent Females (1787); the Friendly Female Society for the Relief of Poor, Infirm, Aged Widows and Single Women of Good Character Who Have Seen Better Days (1802); the euphoniously named Forlorn Female's Fund of Mercy for the Employment of Destitute and Forlorn Females (1812); and the Maritime Female Penitent Refuge for Poor Degraded Females (1829). There were also the Institution for the Protection of Young Country Girls (1801) and, for the girls who escaped the net of those protectors, the Society for Returning Young Women to Their Friends in the Country (founding date unknown).[86]

A representative example of institutions devoted to the uplift of fallen women was the Female Penitentiary for Penitent Prostitutes, founded in 1808 in Stonehouse and later moved to Plymouth.[87] (The three towns that made up greater Plymouth were Plymouth Dock, called Devonport after 1824, Stonehouse, and Plymouth.) The penitentiary was built with private money after investigations revealed the crowded, filthy conditions in the Poor's Portion Workhouse. While the penitentiary was well organized and clean, it was a grim and repressive institution. Newly admitted women were placed in solitary confinement to contemplate their past sins until it was determined that they would not pollute the attitude of the other inmates, who presumably had rejected forever "their lives of shame." Inmates were dressed in drab uniforms, and their heads were shaved to humble their pride in their physical appeal. They were forced into a rigid daily routine in which every hour was accounted for, beginning with prayers at dawn followed by ten or twelve hours of work. The aim of the institution was to teach the inmates a useful skill so that they would be able to find respectable work when they were released. In practice the penitents toiled at the same boring unskilled jobs, such as scrubbing other people's laundry, that workhouse residents performed and that did nothing to improve possibilities for future employment. Most of the penitentiary inmates ran away. The few who were released into respectable jobs were hired as domestic servants, and since it seems likely that many of them had worked as housemaids before they turned to prostitution, this supposed salvation merely put them back where they had started. Data gathered in the 1870s in London showed that 82 percent of the prostitutes in institutions run by the Rescue Society had formerly been house servants, and since by far the greatest number of jobs available to women in Plymouth were in domestic service, a similar pattern was no doubt evident at the Plymouth Penitentiary for Penitent Prostitutes earlier in the century.[88]

Although the reform movement aided some destitute girls and women and eventually led to greater legal protection of young girls against sexual exploitation, the effectiveness of these many institutions was slight, considering the great effort exerted. The reformer James Beard Talbot stated that in the seventy-seven years between 1758 and 1844 not more than fifteen thousand women in London received aid from the organizations set up to help and reform prostitutes, an average of two hundred a year.[89] That is a very small number compared with the thousands of women each year who were living by prostitution. Nonetheless, we should not be too quick to dismiss the efforts of these middle-class reformers who at least attempted to aid the indigent. Most of their middle-class contemporaries were concerned only with seeing to it that the poor did not infringe on their own comfortable lives. As for the gentry, with very few exceptions they dismissed as unimportant the problems of all those who were not of their own kind.

The Reform Campaign within the Navy

In the relatively peaceful period of the 1820s following the close of the American Revolution and the Napoleonic Wars, several naval officers began a campaign to get the prostitutes out of naval ships, and for the first time the general public was made aware of the situation on board naval vessels in port.

The Evangelical Admiral Edward Hawker attempted to get the navy to enforce a ban against accepting prostitutes on board naval vessels, but he met with no success. When he found that the Admiralty "did not want to take any decided measures on the subject," he decided to go public.[90] In 1821 he published an anonymous pamphlet entitled *A Statement Respecting the Prevalence of Certain Immoral Practices in His Majesty's Navy* that described in vivid terms the scenes on board ships full of prostitutes. Although it was addressed to the Admiralty, it was distributed widely. It begins:

> It has become an established practice in the British navy to admit, and even to invite, on board our ships of war, immediately on their arrival in port, as many prostitutes as the men, and, in many cases, the officers, may choose to entertain,...all of whom remain on board, domesticated with the ship's company, men and boys, until they again put to sea. The tendency of this practice is to render a ship of war, while in port, a continual scene of riot and disorder, of obscenity and blasphemy, of drunkenness, lewdness, and debauchery.[91]

The pamphlet goes on to point out the hypocrisy of the navy and even the king in professing to fight immorality while continuing to allow "practices at once so profligate, disgraceful, and destructive." It continues:

There is something in the idea of being *humbugged,* to use a vulgar but significant expression.... What can more wear the air of an attempt of this revolting description than to publish Rules and Regulations, and to issue Royal Proclamations for restraining vice and immorality, and to issue sums of money and institute societies for the distribution of Bibles and Prayerbooks among our seamen, and even appoint chaplains to preach to them, and yet after having done all this, to permit and even sanction the practices which...convert our ships of war into brothels of the very worst description.[92]

Hawker even brought up the taboo subject of buggery, or sodomy, among naval crews. (The term *homosexuality* did not exist.) Although fear of an increase in homosexual activity among naval crews was a prime reason for allowing prostitutes on board, officers avoided the very mention of the subject. Sodomy was one of the few capital offenses in the Royal Navy. Not many cases, however, were brought before naval courts. Officers ignored homosexual incidents among their crews if they could.[93] The very word *sodomy* was such an embarrassment that even in court-martial records, euphe-misms such as "unclean acts" and "crimes against nature" were used.

Hawker, in his efforts to refute all the arguments that could be made in defense of having women on board, argued that the presence of the prostitutes actually encouraged "unnatural crimes" (homosexual acts). "It is," he said, "when a familiarity with gross pollution has prepared the mind for further grossnesses that such enormities [as sodomy] are to be apprehended."[94]

While Hawker provided pages and pages of arguments against allowing prostitutes on board, he scarcely mentioned how the ancient tradition could safely be canceled. His only reference to the need for regular shore leave was presented almost as an aside, in this one sentence: "If reasonable permission were given them (the seamen) to go on shore when circumstances would admit to it, the sailors, grateful for the indulgence, would be more disposed to return to their ships than they are at present."[95]

Admiral Hawker's diatribe reveals the prejudices of gentlemen of his day. He was shocked that surgeon's mates on some ships were "forced to submit to the indignity" of examining for venereal disease the women coming on board; any indignity to the women was below Hawker's notice. While dismissing the feelings of the women of the lower deck, he was solicitous toward officers' wives. He reported the following incident as an example of the way the presence of prostitutes affected the sensibility of a captain's wife: "In a case that has lately occurred, the captain and his wife were actually on the quarterdeck on a Sunday morning while seventy-eight prostitutes were undergoing an inspection of the first lieutenant to ascertain that their dress was clean."[96]

Hawker's anonymous pamphlet caused a sensation, and it almost immediately went into a second printing. The most clear-headed response to its charges came from Captain Anselm Griffiths, who countered Hawker's dramatic outcry with a more temperate approach to the problem of ridding naval ships of prostitutes. In his book on naval economy, published in 1824, Griffiths cautioned that "you cannot make men moral by mere force of authority," and he maintained that women should be banned only if the seamen were given "every liberal indulgence of leave on shore." He pointed out that "the admission of two or three hundred profligate women into the confined space of a ship's between-decks is bad," but since shore leave is denied, "it is a sort of necessity," and "it has to plead long, very long, prescriptive custom." He was even sympathetic toward the prostitutes. "Generally speaking those women do," he wrote, "preserve as fair a portion of decency as you can expect."[97]

Griffiths also disagreed with Hawker regarding the problem of homosexuality in naval crews. It was Griffiths's belief that lack of women did increase cases of sodomy. He pointed out that "during the late war the crime [of sodomy] increased to a _most_ alarming extent," and he suggested that this was due to "the very lengthened periods at sea and the consequent absence of female society."[98]

The first step in abolishing prostitution on board, Griffiths wrote, should be to deny any officer, whether admiral, captain, or lieutenant, the privilege of bringing a woman on board.[99] This was a most unpopular suggestion among most of his fellow officers. Even those who did not bring their own women on board disapproved of any official restrictions on their freedom.

As a result of the reformers' efforts, the subject of prostitutes in naval ships received a great deal of public attention, but neither Parliament nor the Admiralty took any action on the matter, and the public's interest in the subject soon waned.

THE PROSTITUTES RETREAT TO SHORE

The gradual withdrawal of prostitutes from the ships of the Royal Navy was primarily due, not to the reformers' campaign, but to a series of improvements in naval life. These improvements resulted in a drop in desertions that in turn led to greater willingness among officers to give shore leave.

Following the close of the Napoleonic Wars in 1815, the number of seamen was greatly reduced, and it was no longer necessary to use press gangs to fill naval crews. With the demise of impressment, a major cause of desertion was gone, and in a much smaller navy made up of volunteers, captains began to lose their dread of giving shore leave.

By 1826 specific regulations had been established for maintaining clean, ventilated, dry living quarters, and for providing fresh meat and vegetables to naval crews as well as tea and cocoa.[100] With the increase of regular physical examinations and the steady improvement of medical care, the incidence of disease was greatly reduced. Discipline became less harsh and less arbitrary. Pay gradually increased, wages were paid more promptly, and there were more opportunities for advancement. In the 1850s a workable allotment system was instituted.[101]

Ironclad steamships gradually replaced wooden sailing ships—the Battle of Navarino in 1827 was the last great battle fought under sail—and life on board steamships was much less harsh than it had been within the old "wooden walls." Conditions were also much less crowded; wind-driven ships had needed a great number of men to work the sails. While sailing ships could remain at sea for months, steamships had to come into port regularly in order to refuel. This meant that food and water were replenished more frequently, and there were more opportunities for shore leave. Furthermore, since steamships required crews who were trained in technical skills, it was expedient for the navy to improve living conditions and provide better benefits so that men would continue in its service for an extended time after they had been trained for specific skilled jobs. In 1853 the old system of hire and discharge, under which crews were signed up for a single commission only, was replaced by a continuous-service policy. The new policy fostered consistent regulations throughout the navy, in contrast to the former situation in which each vessel's captain had control over his men's lives.

All these changes made for happier, better-disciplined crews whose officers could trust them not to run away when they were allowed to go on shore.

With the drop in desertions and the increase of leave, the long tradition of allowing crowds of women on board faded away. By the 1840s most captains were giving shore leave in home ports, so that crowds of prostitutes seldom came into vessels in English harbors. By the 1850s, even in foreign ports, the practice had become rare.

It was during the 1840s that the following apocryphal story was widely circulated in the navy. When the crew of one of the ships lying at Portsmouth threatened to mutiny because the captain refused to allow women on board, the port admiral signaled the captain of a ship full of prostitutes to send two hundred of the women over to the troubled vessel. He did so, and the mutiny was quelled.[102] This fictitious anecdote was a joke that could only be made at a time when the old tradition had faded. During the 150 years when it was accepted that Royal Navy ships in harbor would be full of prostitutes, the story would have amused neither the officers nor the seamen themselves.

CHAPTER 2

Women of the Lower Deck at Sea

British women served at the same guns with their husbands,
and during a contest of many hours, never shrank from danger,
but animated all around them.

—Admiral Edward Pellew, Viscount Exmouth,
reporting on the Battle of Algiers

NOT ALL THE WOMEN living in naval vessels disembarked when the crowds of prostitutes were sent ashore shortly before the ships sailed. From the late seventeenth century until the middle of the nineteenth, it was customary for wives of warrant officers to go to sea. A warrant officer was assigned to a particular ship "in constant employ," unlike both commissioned officers and seamen, who were signed onto a vessel only for a single commission, and who were often transferred to another ship before the commission was

47

completed. A warrant officer and his wife might continue to live in a ship even when she was taken out of commission.

The wives of the ancient triumvirate of warrant officers—the boatswain, the gunner, and the carpenter—went to sea as a matter of course. So did wives of the purser and the master, who associated with the commissioned officers on the quarterdeck, as well as those of lower rank: the cooper, the sailmaker, and the cook. Petty officers—men who were selected from among the able seamen to direct the less skilled—and a few seamen, usually experienced men who made the navy their career, also sometimes brought their wives to sea.

Very few of the prostitutes who lived on the lower deck in port remained on board when the vessels sailed for foreign stations. A prostitute had little hope of earning money at sea; the men would have spent most of their pay before they sailed from England and would not be paid until they returned. A prostitute "common to the ship's company" had a hard time at sea; a woman was dependent on a man to share his hammock and his food ration with her and to act as her protector.[1]

Most of the women who joined their husbands or sweethearts at sea knew before they went that life on board would be both tedious and perilous, and they realized that they might be away from home for years. Looking back at these women from a modern viewpoint, it is tempting to decide that they went to sea because they wished to find adventure. This was seldom their motivation. The evidence is that wives went to sea because they did not want to be separated from their spouses. Women who joined naval crews disguised as men were often seeking a broader experience than society allowed them on shore. Seagoing wives, on the other hand, did not set out to break social taboos. They were, in fact, behaving as a good wife was supposed to behave: cleaving to her husband and serving as his helpmate, no matter where that took her.

Officially, the women living on the lower deck did not exist. Even when a woman died at sea, the fact was seldom recorded. Their names were not listed in ships' muster books, and since only those people who were mustered had any official existence, women were not paid and not victualed. Wives had to share their husbands' food ration, and so did any children with them. In contrast, soldiers' wives who traveled with their husbands were victualed at two-thirds the men's ration, and their children got half a ration. This meant that in a ship carrying both seamen's and soldiers' wives, the soldiers' wives, who were merely passengers, were given food while the seamen's wives, who were an integral part of the ship's company, got nothing.

THE TRADITION OF WOMEN GOING TO SEA

Women in the King's Ships in the Middle Ages

There is a long history of women going to sea in the king's or queen's ships. In the Middle Ages, when voyages were brief, many of them were prostitutes.

Thomas Walsingham, a fourteenth-century priest, noted in his history of England, the *Historia brevis,* that a number of prostitutes were taken to sea when a fleet under the earl of Buckingham and the duke of Brittany set out on 8 November 1377 to attack the Spanish fleet. On 11 November many of the smaller ships foundered in a gale, and their people had to be transferred to the larger vessels. The remains of the fleet limped back to port for repairs, then set out again with the prostitutes still on board. After searching futilely for the enemy up and down the channel, the English finally met the Spanish fleet off Brest. Buckingham captured eight ships, but the rest of the Spaniards escaped, and the battle was considered a failure. More bad weather was met with, and it was after Christmas when the fleet finally got back home. According to the pious Walsingham, the failure and ordeals of the expedition were

God's retribution against the sailors for having taken "public women" to sea with them.[2]

The remarkable number of sixty women were on board Sir John Arundel's ships when they set out from Southampton in December 1379 to go to the aid of the duke of Brittany, then fighting in Brittany. Some of the women went willingly—they were probably prostitutes—but the rest were "married women, widows, and young ladies of rank" who were kidnapped from an abbey near Southampton where many of Arundel's men had been quartered while the fleet waited for the weather to improve. At length Arundel grew so impatient to be off that even though a new storm was brewing, he gave orders to sail. A gale struck the ships off the coast of Cornwall, and it seemed that the whole fleet would be wrecked. As the wind continued to mount, the terrified men became convinced that the storm was a supernatural one, caused by the presence of the women. According to a long-held superstition, even one woman at sea could bring forth a fatal storm, and they had sixty with them. All sixty women were thrown overboard.[3] The remedy failed. The storm continued to threaten the fleet, and twenty-five of Arundel's ships were wrecked on islands off the Irish coast. Most of the men, including Arundel and Rust, died.

Women in Naval Ships in the Seventeenth Century

By the seventeenth century the tradition of seagoing wives was well established. Phineas Pett, famous master shipwright and naval commissioner, reporting on the wreck of the *Anne Royal* on 10 April 1637, noted that among the people drowned were the master's wife and another woman, and there is no indication that Pett found it unusual that the women had been on board.[4]

In 1674 a naval captain got into trouble as a result of having women in his ship, but only because they were costing the government money. In that year a government informer named Jones notified the Admiralty that the captain of the *Ruby* had listed two seamen's wives in his ship's muster book under male names so that he himself could pocket their pay. Jones also reported that the captain of the *Thomas and Francis* had collected the pay of a "Mr. Bromley," who was in fact the captain's dog.[5] So far as the navy was concerned, the women and the dog were in the same category. One is reminded of Horatio Nelson's memorandum announcing that before he sailed he was determined to rid his ship "of all the women, dogs, and pigeons."[6]

Admiralty Regulations

The Admiralty's first printed *Regulations and Instructions,* issued in 1731, stated, "[A captain] is not to carry any women to sea…without orders from the Admiralty." Later editions of the *Regulations* reiterated this order, with the added proviso that permission could be granted by an admiral without Admiralty approval.[7] While official permission was often granted for captains' wives and other "ladies" to live in the officers' quarters of ships at sea, instances of warrant officers' or seamen's wives being authorized to go to sea were few and far between. They did occur, however.

In 1819, when the duke and duchess of Clarence and the two Ladies Fitz-Clarence were preparing to embark for Antwerp in His Majesty's Yacht *Royal Sovereign,* the Admiralty ordered that "a respectable woman, sufficiently used to the sea," should be hired to attend the ladies and should be entered on the books as an able seaman. A Mrs. Davis, the wife of a Greenwich Hospital pensioner, carried out the assignment.[8]

The Royal Navy operated as much by unwritten tradition as by written regulations, and the tradition of taking women to sea was firmly established by the eighteenth century. Even the sparse instructions given in the *Regulations and Instructions* were often ignored. Captains were given a great deal of latitude in running their ships according to their own rules, and while they grumbled about the women of the lower deck, most of them accepted the women's presence as inevitable and simply carried on as though the women did not exist.

The Admiralty did the same. Only when it was officially informed of a women's presence in a ship at sea did it take action. The navy was forced to take notice when evidence was presented in the court-martial of Captain Marriot Arbuthnot of the *Guarland* on 13 March 1755 that he had carried the wives of the master and boatswain to sea, and he was reprimanded, but this infringement of the regulations would have passed unnoticed if it had not been mentioned in the testimony given before the court.[9]

One of the few admirals who flatly refused to allow women in his ships at sea was Cuthbert Collingwood. He was so opposed to the practice that were it not for his reputation as a pragmatist, one might suspect him of believing that women at sea were bad luck. In 1808, when he heard there was a woman on board the *Pickle,* he sent an order to Rear Admiral Purvis: "I never knew a woman brought to sea in a ship that some mischief did not befall the vessel. If she did not go home [to England] with the lieutenant, pray send her out of the fleet in the first transport or merchant ship going home. She must pay her passage."[10]

The following year Collingwood was greatly dismayed when he found women in his own flagship. He later explained: "Captain Carden had given permission for a number of women to come in this ship [the *Ville de Paris*]. I have reproved him for this irregularity and considering the mischief they never fail to create wherever they are, I have ordered them all on board the *Ocean* to be conveyed to England again."[11]

The Daily Routine of Wives at Sea

Seamen and their wives had neither privacy nor quiet on board. They shared one hammock squeezed among hundreds of others in the great open space of the lower deck. At sea there was slightly more space for sleeping than there was in port when the fourteen to sixteen inches allowed each hammock was occupied throughout the night. At sea the hammocks of the men standing watch were empty

C. Mosley's line engraving of 1743 is a highly romanticized view of the lower deck, showing a gunport the size of a large window. The opening was actually only large enough for the gun to extend through it. From Charles N. Robinson, *The British Tar in Fact and Fiction* (New York and London: Harper and Brothers, 1909), facing 6. BOSTON ATHENAEUM part of the night, allowing their neighbors more room. A third or more of the men, however, did not stand watch; the "idlers" slept through the night unless all hands were called. (The term *idler* was applied to the men who did not keep watches but assisted the carpenter or the sailmaker or worked in the hold or did numerous other jobs during the day; they were far from idle.)[12]

Warrant officers' wives had a little more privacy than seamen's wives, since they shared their husbands' small canvas-sided cabins located on the sides of the lower deck. In some vessels the cabins of the gunner and boatswain were on the orlop deck, below the lower deck. The orlop was the lowest deck, below the water line, where the surgeon's quarters and the storerooms were. It was even darker and more oppressive there, but quieter than among the hordes crowded together on the lower deck.

The nightly routine of everyone on board revolved around the system of dividing the crew into two alternating watches. Each watch was four hours long. One watch slept from 8:00 P.M. until midnight, when they rose and went on deck and the men of the other watch turned in. At four in the morning there was another scramble as the sleeping men were awakened and made their way through the dark to their stations.[13] And if there was a sudden shift in the wind or another crisis, all hands were called. Even the women's sleep was never sustained.

By around 8:00 A.M. the whole ship was up, all hammocks were stowed away, and every man went to his assigned task. All the men were busy from early in the morning until late afternoon, except for the times allotted for breakfast and for the midday issue of grog followed by dinner. The only task of the wives was to keep out of the way of the work going on throughout the ship.

Warrant officers' wives were better off than the wives of the seamen in many ways; they not only had a cabin to retire to, and could even have some of their own furniture with them, but they also were more likely to know how to read and write than seamen's wives and so could pass long days in writing letters and reading.

(Their husbands had to be literate in order to keep records of the supplies they were in charge of.) There were few books available, however; books were expensive, and there was little space for storing them. During the nineteenth century, Evangelical captains provided the men with Bibles and religious tracts, but even these were lacking in earlier times.

Warrant officers' wives enjoyed the services of one or two servants who polished shoes, ran errands, and prepared special dishes. Most of the servants were boys, often only eleven or twelve years old. A warrant officer's wife often formed a close maternal relationship with the child assigned to her husband. The wife of William Richardson, the gunner of the fifty-four-gun *Tromp*, grew very fond of her husband's servant, a young boy who was assigned to Richardson after he was found stowed away following the *Tromp*'s visit to Madeira in 1800 on her way to the West Indies. Mrs. Richardson and the boy were both heartbroken when later he was transferred to the fleet's flagship to serve as one of the admiral's servants.[14]

A seaman's wife had no place of her own, and the only personal belongings she had with her were the few things she could store in her husband's sea chest. Wives spent their days in small groups, sometimes on the relatively quiet orlop deck or, in cold weather, near the galley on the lower deck, where the stove provided the only heat in the ship. They might do some sewing, although the men themselves were skilled at making their own clothes.

Some seamen's wives, when they got the chance, obtained a tub of water and did some laundry, not only for their husbands but for other seamen willing to pay a few pence for the service. At sea, where drinking water was in short supply, laundry was supposed to be done in salt water, which meant that the clothes never quite dried—a problem that contributed to the men's discomfort and rheumatic ills. Whenever they dared, the women washed with some of the supply of fresh water (a misnomer; it was always rank). Admiral John Jervis, earl of St. Vincent, was obsessed with the idea that the women in his fleet squandered the drinking water. He waged a long but futile campaign against the women who, he said, "still infest His Majesty's ships in great numbers, and who *will* have water to wash, that they and their reputed husbands may get drunk on the earnings."[15]

On 14 July 1796 Jervis circulated the following peevish memorandum to his captains from H.M.S. *Victory,* at sea. In one remarkably long sentence he cautioned:

> There being reason to apprehend that a number of women have been clandestinely brought from England in several ships,…the respective captains are required by the admiral to admonish those ladies upon the waste of water and other disorders committed by them, and to make known to all that on the first proof of water being obtained for washing, from the scuttlebutt [a cask of drinking water placed on deck for the use of the crew] or otherwise, under false pretences, in any ship, every woman in the fleet who has not been admitted under the authority of the Admiralty or the commander-in-chief will be shipped for England by the first convoy.[16]

The order was ignored. A year elapsed, and still Jervis fretted about the women wasting water. On 21 June 1797 he sent another memorandum to his captains in which he announced, in another long grandiloquent sentence, that the future of England rested on whether or not the women could be prevented from using drinking water to wash clothes:

> Observing as I do with the deepest concern the great deficiency of water in several ships of the squadron, which cannot have happened without waste by collusion, and the service of our king and country requiring that the blockade of Cadiz, on which depends a speedy and honourable peace, should be continued, an event impracticable without the strictest economy in the expenditure of water, it will become my indispensable duty to land all the women in the squadron at Gibraltar, unless this alarming evil is not immediately corrected.[17]

Rear Admiral Nelson, serving in the *Theseus* under Jervis, was on friendly enough terms with his superior to dare to suggest that Jervis would be wise to temper his anger. Nelson responded to Jervis's memorandum the same day:

> The history of women was brought forward I remember in the channel fleet last war. I know not if your ship was an exception, but I will venture to say not an Honourable [a captain] but had plenty of them, and they always will do as they please. Orders are not for them—at least I never yet knew one who obeyed.[18]

Nelson did not mention the possibility that sending the wives home might inflame the seamen; there was currently disaffection throughout the navy. The mutiny at Spithead had been resolved only in May, and the mutiny at the Nore had ended only the previous week. Apparently Jervis accepted Nelson's admonition and did not carry out his threat to send the women off.

While most commissioned officers disliked having lower-deck women in their ships at sea, they enjoyed having "ladies of quality" traveling in the officers' quarters. Jervis and Nelson were no exception. At the same time that Jervis sent off his complaining memorandum of 14 July 1796, he was enjoying the company of the socially prominent Mr. and Mrs. Wynne and their four daughters, who lived for several months in the ships of his fleet after being evacuated from Leghorn at the approach of Napoleon's army. Jervis was especially fond of the pretty teenagers Betsey and Jenny Wynne. He nicknamed them the Admirables, and he and his officers entertained them at a round of dinner parties and dances. Jervis also promoted the engagement of Betsey to one of his captains, Thomas Fremantle.[19]

After Betsey Wynne married Fremantle she lived on board her husband's ship in Nelson's squadron with the full approval of Nelson. Nelson also took Lord and Lady Hamilton on a cruise in the spring of 1801 in the *Foudroyant* from Palermo to Syracuse and

Malta and back. It was during this pleasant interlude that Horatia, the daughter of Emma Hamilton and Nelson, was conceived. (The cruise was made between 23 April and 30 May 1801; Horatia was born sometime between 29 January and 5 February 1802.)[20]

Meals on the Lower Deck

A seaman's wife joined her husband and his messmates on the lower deck for all meals. Each mess contained some six to eight men who ate from a common pot at a table suspended from the rafters in a space against the side of the ship between two guns. The food was usually plentiful but monotonous, consisting primarily of boiled salt meat, hard biscuits, and dried peas, varying little from meal to meal. There was no coffee, tea, or hot chocolate served, which would have been a comfort in cold weather in the unheated ship. In most vessels breakfast was at eight, two hours after the hammocks had been stowed and the men had scrubbed the decks. Half the grog ration was served before dinner at noon, and the other half before supper at five.

The men themselves selected who would join their mess, and messmates were bonded together, sharing their free time and defending one another against outsiders. It is somewhat surprising that these tightly knit groups accepted a woman among them, but there is no indication that a seaman's wife was not welcomed. Mary Lacy, who served in the navy as William Chandler, described convivial meals in her mess on board the *Royal Sovereign* in 1760, which included the female companion of one of the seamen.[21]

Warrant officers' wives ate better than the seamen's wives. Wives of warrant officers of wardroom rank—the master, the purser, the chaplain, and the surgeon—ate with the commissioned officers, sharing their delicacies and good wine. The boatswain, the carpenter, and the gunner and their wives ate separately from the seamen, and they too often supplemented ship's rations with fresh meat and wine, tea, and coffee. The gunner William Richardson and his wife

An inaccurate but charming woodcut showing a seaman
and his wife from an early-nineteenth-century broadside
ballad. From John Ashton, ed., *Modern Street Ballads*
(London: Chatto and Windus, 1888), 223. BOSTON
ATHENAEUM

brought several pigs on board on their passage home from the West
Indies, and they shared the last of the roast pork with other warrant
officers, and with "the poor women" (soldiers' wives) as well as an
army sergeant. (Richardson charged the latter for his portion.)[22]

Recreation and Entertainment

Each day in the late afternoon, captains allowed their men time to
relax. In good weather, wives joined the seamen on the open main
deck to dance and "to skylark" (to indulge in horseplay and active
games such as "follow my leader"). They danced to the music of the
ship's fiddler or were accompanied by another instrument; bag-
pipes were popular.[23] In heavy weather, however, the women were

constrained to the lower deck, where, with the gunports closed, the only light and air came from the main hatchway. While the men got fresh air working in the rigging and on the main deck, the women spent most of their time below in the odoriferous dark.

Wives also participated in the plays that crews organized and performed for their officers. Early in 1813, when Britain was at war with both the United States and France, the American diplomat Mordecai Noah witnessed such a production on board the seventy-four-gun *Bulwark,* flagship of Rear Admiral Philip Charles Durham on blockade off Rochefort. Noah had been on his way to his post as United States consul at Tunis, by way of France, when the American merchant schooner he was traveling in was captured by the English frigate *Briton,* Captain Thomas Staines, one of the ships in Durham's fleet, and Noah was taken prisoner. His was not an onerous incarceration. Sir Thomas treated him as an honored guest, showed him around the *Briton,* and gave him the use of his own library. Admiral Durham invited Noah to visit the *Bulwark* for dinner, and a five-act play entitled "Wild Oats" was performed by the crew, followed by a group of seamen dancing the hornpipe, accompanied by the ship's band. The play was well acted, and the scenery included "drop curtains, stage doors with knockers, footlights, and all the paraphernalia necessary to a well-organized and well-governed stage." But for Noah the high point of the entertainment was watching one particular dancer, "an interesting figure, tastefully dressed, and moving on the light fantastic toe with much ease and agility." Noah later reported in his journal the admiral's comment to him:

> "Don't stare so," said the admiral, "it is a *real* woman, the wife of a foretop man. We are compelled in a fleet to have a few women to wash and mend, etc."
>
> The sight of a *real* woman, as the admiral called her, was refreshing after a long voyage, particularly as the female parts in "Wild Oats" were awkwardly sustained by men.[24]

Childbirth

Childbirth was not an unusual occurrence at sea. It was always difficult. Children were often born in the midst of a battle or in bad weather, but even in quiet times there was no comfortable place for the birth to occur. The storerooms on the orlop deck provided the most privacy, but these rooms were not readily available; the warrant officer in charge had to be persuaded to give over the key. Births often took place on one of the tables between two guns on the lower deck, with only some canvas draped across to provide a modicum of privacy. From this situation comes the phrase "son of a gun," a euphemism for "son of a bitch," the assumption being that a child born between two guns on the lower deck was illegitimate, although in fact this was not usually the case.

There is an interesting anecdote concerning a child born in the United States ship *Chesapeake* during the Barbary Wars. (Seamen's wives went to sea in the American navy as they did in all the major navies of the period.) The wife of seaman James Low, captain of the forecastle, bore a son in the boatswain's storeroom on 22 February 1803, the day after the vessel sailed from Algiers. The baby was named for a midshipman, Melancthon Woolsey, who was godfather when the child was baptized by the ship's chaplain on 31 March, and following the baptism Woolsey provided "a handsome collation of wine and fruit." Mrs. Low was sick and could not attend the christening, so Mrs. Hays, the gunner's wife, officiated. Either Woolsey did not extend his friendship to the other women on board or there was dissension among them, for the wives of the boatswain, the carpenter, and the corporal were not invited and "got drunk in their own quarters, out of pure spite."[25]

Sexual Harassment

From the sparse records available, it appears that there was very little sexual harassment of the women. The warrant officers' wives were safer from unwanted sexual overtures than seamen's wives;

a man would think twice before accosting his superior's spouse. But the seamen's wives also were fairly safe. The surprising evidence is that seamen, although they endured months or even years of celibate existence on board, usually left their shipmates' wives alone. This was partly because a woman's husband and his friends would make life miserable for a man who accosted the woman. It was also partly because the men were closely supervised around the clock. During the day they were under the eyes of the officers directing them in their work. At night there was usually an hourly check of the lower deck, primarily to establish that there was no unguarded light that could start a fire, but also to make sure that no disorder was occurring. All the same, there were times when a man off duty could find a woman alone in an unfrequented part of the ship; we know that homosexual activity went on despite the lack of privacy. Undoubtedly there were cases of women being sexually harassed that went unreported, but if incidents had been common, there surely would have been some mention of them in letters and journals.

I have found one instance of a woman attempting adultery but failing in the attempt: the case of the cuckolded coxswain. In the sloop *Petrel,* cruising off the coast of Greece in 1796, the coxswain's wife, while her husband was away with some officers exploring the shoreline, was seen in cozy concourse with a seaman. The boat party, however, returned sooner than she expected, and the illicit affair was interrupted.[26]

The only example I know of a wife being raped occurred during a mutiny when both discipline and social restraints had been overthrown. This singular case took place in the thirty-two-gun frigate *Hermione* in the early-morning hours of 21 September 1797, after Captain Hugh Pigot and most of his officers had been murdered by the mutineers.[27] Richard Redman, a twenty-four-year-old quartermaster's mate, after joining in the slaughter of the captain and other officers, carried out a premeditated attack on the boatswain's wife, the only woman on board.[28] First he raided the officers' wine supply and consumed a great quantity of Madeira. He then went down to the cabin of the boatswain, William Martin, where Martin and his wife were cowering. Redman was heard to shout, "By the Holy Ghost, the Boatswain shall go with the rest." He then crashed into the cabin, grabbed Martin, and forced him up to the main deck, where he pushed him through a gunport to drown. He then returned to Mrs. Martin in the cabin, carrying more bottles of Madeira, "and was not seen again that night."[29]

It is interesting that as violent as the *Hermione* mutineers were—they killed ten officers, including one in the last stages of yellow fever, whom they dragged from his bed and threw overboard—none of the men besides Redman tried to assault Mrs. Martin either during the mutiny or in the following days when they were taking the vessel to the enemy's port of La Guaira on the Spanish Main.

At La Guaira the ship was given over to the Spanish, and the crew dispersed. Redman joined a Spanish merchant ship that was later captured by the British, whereupon he was identified as one of the *Hermione* mutineers and sent to Portsmouth to be court-martialed. In March 1799, on board the *Gladiator* at Portsmouth, although he claimed he was innocent of any wrongdoing, Redman was found guilty and sentenced to death; he was executed an hour after the close of the court-martial.[30] In the evidence given at the court-martial, the only time Mrs. Martin was mentioned was when the captain's steward testified that Redman had spent the night with her. All that is known about her following the *Hermione*'s arrival at La Guaira is that she took passage in a ship bound for the United States, hoping no doubt to get back to England from there. (She could not travel directly to England from an enemy port.)

WOMEN AT SEA FACING CRISES AND DEATH

Captain William Henry Dillon praised the women in his ship the *Horatio* for their help in saving the vessel when, in May 1815, she struck a rock off the island of Guernsey and tore a hole in her bottom. The vessel floated off, but water was pouring in through the opening. While the crew worked the pumps, a group of their wives quickly set to work "thrumming a sail" (sewing on strips of oakum to thicken it), which was then passed down the ship's side and over the hole. This stanched the leak sufficiently to allow the vessel to get to Portsmouth for repairs. Unfortunately, in the process of getting the sail overboard, a boatswain's mate, whose wife was present, fell into the water. A boat was lowered to help him, but the crew of the ship were terrified that if they delayed, they would all be lost. They pleaded with Captain Dillon: "Only one man, sir; we are upward of three hundred. Pray save us. We have no time to lose." After several minutes the search was abandoned. The man's wife, Dillon remarked, "was in sad distress at her loss."[31]

In a rare instance when the wife of a newly impressed man went to sea, her sea experience was harrowing from beginning to end. The woman—her name is not recorded—was in the last month of pregnancy when she went on board the twenty-eight-gun *Proserpine,* Captain James Wallis, at Yarmouth to bid her husband goodbye. The ship was suddenly ordered to sea and sailed before the woman could return to shore. On 28 January 1799 the *Proserpine* headed into the North Sea bound for Cuxhaven near the mouth of the Elbe River to drop off the Honorable Thomas Grenville, a government official on his way to deliver important documents to Berlin. That same day the woman gave birth to a dead child.[32]

By late afternoon of the thirty-first the ship was within four miles of Cuxhaven when a gale came up, and there was such heavy snow that it was impossible to see to navigate further up the river. They were obliged to drop anchor. The following morning, ice had blocked the way into Cuxhaven. Captain Wallis stood out to sea, hoping to put Mr. Grenville ashore on the coast of Jutland. Heavy winds continued, and the *Proserpine* had only reached the mouth of the river when she was blown onto a sandbank. The crew attempted to get her off, but it was impossible for them to continue working in the bitter weather. By the following dawn, ice was up to the cabin windows, and everyone was suffering from the intense cold. (Vessels of that time were not heated.)

Captain Wallis realized that the only hope of saving his people was to abandon the ship and get everyone to the nearest village on the island of Newark, six miles away. They set out across the ice, blinded by snow and struggling to keep on their feet in the high wind, sometimes clambering over boulders of ice, at other times struggling through water up to their waists.

The only other woman on board was another seaman's wife, "a strong healthy woman accustomed to the hardships of a maritime life," carrying her nine-month-old child. She was not as sturdy as she appeared; both she and her baby died on the way to the village. Twelve seamen also died of exposure. The impressed man's wife survived.[33]

Many wives went to the West Indies even though they knew in advance that they were likely to die of yellow fever. In July 1800 the old fifty-four-gun two-decker *Tromp* carried thirteen women and a female toddler to Martinique. The *Tromp*'s gunner, William Richardson, who described the voyage in his journal, had tried to persuade his wife to stay at home, but she "had fixed her mind to go," and at length he gave his consent, "especially as the captain's, the master's, the purser's, and boatswain's wives were going with them; and the serjeant of marines and six other men's wives had leave [from their husbands] to go." The captain's wife brought her maid, and the boatswain and his wife brought their two infants. "A person," Richardson commented, "would have thought they were all insane wishing to go to such a sickly country!"[34]

The *Tromp* arrived in the harbor of Port Royal in Martinique after a six-week passage during which the captain's wife gave birth to a son. It was not long after their arrival that the fever struck with a vengeance. "Every day," Richardson reported, "we were sending people to the hospital, and few returned." Among the first to die were the master and his wife, "large in a family way." "Next died Mr. Campbell, the boatswain, leaving a wife and son and daughter on board."[35] Only three of the thirteen women survived: Mrs. Richardson, the boatswain's widow, and the captain's wife. (The wife of the captain was able to return to England not long after her arrival, but the other two women had no way to escape.)

Richardson's wife almost succumbed to the fever; she would have died if she had not been carefully nursed. Rather than send her to the crowded, insanitary hospital, Richardson hired an airy room in the private house of a skilled nurse, a black woman, who provided constant care and efficacious herbal teas. He also found a French doctor who had spent most of his eighty years in the West Indies and so was familiar with yellow fever; the English doctors knew next to nothing about the disease.

Upon Mrs. Richardson's recovery she and her husband continued to live in the *Tromp* under the most difficult circumstances. The ship had been converted into a prison ship and was now crammed with former French slaves. For two years the Richardsons, together with the few remaining officers and crew, were crowded into one small area at the stern of the main deck, the only space not filled with prisoners. The prisoners were desperate men, and there was the constant danger that they would take over the ship and murder the English on board. Prisoners escaped almost every night; the ship's sides were so rotten that it was easy for them to loosen the bolts that held the ports shut. Mrs. Richardson, on the other hand, seldom got on shore since her husband only rarely got leave, even though he was a warrant officer, and it was dangerous for her to go alone.

At last, two years after her arrival in Port Royal, the *Tromp* was readied for sea, and she returned to Portsmouth on 5 September 1802. Mrs. Richardson's friends in Portsmouth, who had heard that both she and her husband had died in the West Indies, "received her as one risen from the dead." She did not go to sea again.[36]

Widows and Widows' Men

William Richardson reported in his journal that when the *Tromp's* boatswain died, he left a wife and two children on board, but he does not say what happened to them. Other sea journals are equally silent about the fate of a woman who became widowed on board. If her ship was not returning soon to England, she was apparently sent home in another naval vessel. No contemporary source explains how she managed on the voyage home without a man to sponsor her. Who hung her hammock each night and stowed it away each morning? She would not have been allowed to join the men in this duty. How did she feed herself and her children? No one tells us.

The widow of a man who had died of disease was worse off than one whose husband had been killed in action or in a shipboard accident. When a man died accidentally or in battle, his clothing and other effects were auctioned off and the proceeds given to his widow, but this could not be done if a man died of a contagious disease, or at least we hope not.

A seaman's widow was entitled to her husband's back pay when his ship was eventually paid off, but she seldom managed to get through the red tape necessary to get it. Many widows also failed to get the small pension due them because the process of obtaining it was so complicated. The widows of men killed in major battles sometimes received money from private benefactors or from funds raised by public subscription, but there was no such remuneration for widows of men who died of disease.

Widows were aided by a most curious system, one of the more bizarre traditions of the sailing navy. From 1733 onward, in every commissioned vessel's muster book there were listed two "widows' men" for every hundred men in the crew. They were rated as able seamen. The pay of these nonexistent men was collected in a pension fund for widows. The system, known as "dead shares," was introduced during the reign of Henry VIII for the widows of commissioned and warrant officers. In 1695 it was diverted to the widows of seamen killed in action, and from 1733 onward it was paid for any man who died on board. It was not until 1829 that a less irregular pension system finally replaced it. In earlier centuries fictitious names were given to these ghostly ratings, but starting in the mid-eighteenth century the simple designation "widow's man" was used.[37]

Widows' men were the direct opposite of wives at sea: the wives were alive and present on board but were not mustered and so received no pay; the widows' men did not exist but were listed in the muster book and paid.

Women Mustered in Hospital Ships

There was one situation in the Royal Navy in which women were actually mustered, victualed, and paid. This exception to the rule of male-only naval crews was instituted in the seventeenth century, when it was ordered that women were to be hired to serve in hospital ships as nurses and laundresses. In 1696 each of the six existing hospital ships was to be assigned six nurses and four laundresses. To allay fears that the women would seduce the medical staff or the patients, it was suggested that none of them should be under the age of fifty, and they were to be seamen's wives or widows.[38] They were paid able seamen's wages. The job of nurse had little in common with the nursing profession of today. At that time nurses needed no medical skills; they merely fed and cleaned up the patients and changed the bed linen—when there was bed linen, that is.

There were continual complaints from the officers of the hospital ships that the women were drunk and disorderly, but then there were also complaints of the male assistants' drunkenness. It is not surprising that both male and female workers escaped the misery of their surroundings in drink. Hospital ships were not pleasant places to live and work; they were usually worn-out sixth-rates or old and grimy converted merchant vessels. If they went to sea, they wallowed along behind the faster ships assigned to fight the enemy. There was usually only one surgeon aboard, about four surgeon's mates, six nurses, four laundresses, a cook, and enough crew to work the vessel. The ships were jammed full of desperately sick men, often men with contagious diseases. The female nurses and laundresses had a difficult time, since they were especially vulnerable to sexual harassment and verbal abuse, having no husbands or other male protectors on board to defend them.

A 1743 plan of the gun deck of the hospital ship *Blenheim* indicates what life was like for the nurses.[39] While the lieutenant, the surgeon, and the surgeon's mates lived on the upper deck away from the patients, the nurses were housed in small cabins within the wards, separated from the sick men only by canvas bulkheads. The wards in the *Blenheim* were designated as follows: two for ague (malaria), two itchy wards (for diseases affecting the skin), two fever wards (for a wide range of contagious diseases that might include typhus, typhoid, yellow fever, and cholera), a ward for recovering fever patients, and one for flux (dysentery) patients. In the bow were two large storerooms "for dead men's cloaths." Why these clothes were saved is not clear. Surely this contaminated clothing was not auctioned off to seamen as was the clothing of those slain in fighting ships.

The Admiralty's policy of hiring women for hospital ships was a matter of debate, and feelings ran high on both sides. Some felt that the female nurses provided the patients with a form of nurturing that only women could give. Others were convinced that female nurses were less responsible than their male counterparts.

A complaint was brought before the Admiralty on 10 January 1703 charging that the female nurses of the hospital ship *Princess Anne*, lying at Woolwich, "have done little or no service the last year but are continually drunk as often as opportunity would permit— and then very mutinous."[40] In response, the Admiralty sent Rear

Admiral George Byng and Daniel Furzer, surveyor of the navy, to investigate conditions in the *Princess Anne*. In their report of 24 January 1703 they said that the captain and the surgeon of that ship told them that the female nurses on board "take up a great deal of room and are rather an inconvenience than otherwise."[41] Byng and Furzer recommended that the women be replaced by men.

The Admiralty, as usual, kept its options open. On 26 January it ruled that women would not be hired to serve in hospital ships, but it added the provision "except when circumstances required." Such circumstances quickly developed. On 9 March 1703 three laundresses were hired when the *Princess Anne* was ordered to the Mediterranean.[42] (Five additional nurses were also hired, and they too may have been female.) Again in 1705, five women were hired at Portsmouth to serve on a hospital ship ordered to the Mediterranean where "such persons are not commonly to be had."[43]

The *Regulations and Instructions* of 1731 called for four washerwomen in each hospital ship. At Portsmouth in 1747 the hospital ship *Apollo*, on her way to India in the squadron of Admiral Edward Boscawen, mustered seven women as supernumeraries to assist the surgeon. They served for several years on the India station, and all but one of them was on board in 1749 when the *Apollo* was wrecked on the coast of Coromandel. The six women, together with most of the crew, perished. The one nurse who escaped the disaster was Hannah Giles, who had been sent back to England in the *Harwich* for undisclosed reasons shortly before the wreck of the *Apollo*.[44]

Female nurses were assigned to hospital ships throughout the Seven Years' War (1756–63), although their presence was often resented. In 1759, for example, Dr. Garlick, surgeon of the hospital ship *Princess Caroline*, complained to the Sick and Hurt Board that the ship's commander, Lieutenant Powell, regularly consumed a bottle of gin and then proceeded to "damn the nurses as bitches and threaten to tow them on shore."[45]

Few if any female nurses served in hospital ships after the close of the Seven Years' War. Laundresses continued to be hired in the latter part of the eighteenth century, but by the nineteenth century they too were gone.

Female nurses began serving on shore in 1754, when the earliest section of Haslar Hospital, the first naval hospital, opened. Like their seagoing counterparts, these women were repeatedly condemned for drunkenness and insubordination, and in 1854 they were replaced. They were, however, reinstated in 1885.[46]

WOMEN IN BATTLE

Women played two traditional roles in battle: they assisted the surgeon and his mates in patching up the wounded, and they carried powder to the guns from the magazine, a job shared with the young boys in the crew known as powder-monkeys.

John Nicol, a seaman in the seventy-four-gun _Goliath_, Captain Thomas Foley, reported on the women of that ship at the Battle of the Nile, 1 August 1798. In this great English victory Admiral Horatio Nelson's fleet roundly defeated Napoleon's ships, opening the attack at dusk as the French fleet lay at anchor in Aboukir Bay. The _Goliath_ opened the action, passing through the line of French ships and anchoring on the land side of them. This battle was especially hellish because it was fought at close quarters at night, lighted only by the flash of the guns and the flames from the burning French ships. Nicol wrote:

> My station was in the powder magazine with the gunner. As we entered the bay, we stripped to our trowsers, opened our ports, cleared, and every ship we passed, gave them a broadside and three cheers. Any information we got was from the boys and women who carried the powder. The women behaved as well as the men and got a present for their bravery from the Grand Signior.[47]

Nicol was misinformed on this point. It is true that following the battle a purse of two thousand sequins (coins equal to about nine hundred English pounds) was delivered to Lord Nelson from the Turkish sultan (always called the Grand Signior) to be distributed among the wounded seamen, but it is most unlikely that any women were among the recipients.[48]

Carrying gunpowder was strenuous and nerve-racking work. A woman had to clamber down the ladder from the decks to the powder room deep in the bowels of the ship, slide past the wet curtain that protected the stored powder from sparks, and grab a leather cartridge of powder. She then raced back up the ladders clutching the heavy cartridge, ran along the sand-strewn but still blood-slippery deck through the choking smoke and deafening gunfire to her assigned gun, deposited the cartridge, and once again ran down to the hold for another load. This work continued throughout the battle, since it was dangerous to keep a large supply of powder near the guns.

Nicol continued his report of the women:

> I was much indebted to the gunner's wife who gave her husband and me a drink of wine every now and then, which lessened our fatigue much.
>
> There were some of the women wounded, and one woman belonging to Leith died of her wounds and was buried on a small island in the bay. One woman bore a son in the heat of the action; she belonged to Edinburgh.[49]

Childbirth during Battle

It was not unusual for a woman to give birth during battle; the noise and vibrations of the guns—not to mention the stress—brought on labor. It is impossible to imagine a worse situation in which to bear a child. The ship was cleared for action, all the furniture and partitions were stored away, and there was no one to aid the mother. There was, obviously, no help available from the surgeon or his mates; the surgeon's quarters were crowded with the wounded

Woodcut of a seaman's wife in the midst of battle clutching her child while she helps a wounded seaman. From *The Log Book; or, Nautical Miscellany* (London: J. and W. Robins, 1830), 33. BOSTON ATHENAEUM

waiting their turn to be treated. The services of the women assigned to the surgeon were sorely needed, but perhaps one of them was allowed to assist the woman in childbirth in another part of the orlop deck. Remarkably, in all the instances I have found of births during battle, both mother and newborn survived.

Women Mustered after the Battle

The names of four of the women in the *Goliath* at the Battle of the Nile were actually listed in the muster book two days after the battle; they served as nurses for a period of four months. The muster book notes that they were "victualed at two-third allowance in consideration of their assistance in dressing and attending on the wounded, being widows of men slain in the fight with the enemy on the first day of August."[50]

The widows had no time to mourn the loss of their husbands; they were immediately ordered to continue to nurse the wounded at the close of the battle. In the intense heat of an Egyptian summer, this was a grueling task. (Most of the fleet had left Egypt with Nelson at the close of the fighting, but the *Goliath* and several other ships, their wounded still on board, were left behind to blockade the Egyptian coast.) Sarah Bates's and Mary French's husbands died during the battle, and their bodies were thrown through a gunport into the sea. Ann Taylor's husband lingered for a week, and the husband of Elizabeth Moore did not die until 31 August, a month after the battle.

There is no record of when the four widows were able to return to England, for in the *Goliath*'s muster book the place, date, and reason for discharge of each woman have been carefully erased. There was something about their discharge that the *Goliath*'s officers wished to hide, but unfortunately there is no way to know what irregularity they were covering up.

Christina White was also present at the Battle of the Nile, and she too nursed the wounded for several months following the battle, but the captain of her ship, the *Majestic,* was not so generous as Captain Foley, and she was not mustered. Upon her return to England, White wrote a letter to Admiral Nelson explaining that she was left a widow with two children, and she asked for his help. "Your petitioner," she wrote, "hopes that your Lordship will consider her worthy of your notice, since she attended the surgeon and nursed the wounded on the voyage home for a period of eleven weeks."[51] There is no record of any answer to her letter.

The Horrors of the Surgeon's Quarters

Twenty-nine years after the Battle of the Nile, the role of women in battle had not changed. The seaman Charles M'Pherson wrote about the women in the *Genoa* at the Battle of Navarino, fought on 20 October 1827:

> Nine of our petty officers had wives aboard who were occupied with the doctor and his mates in the cockpit, assisting in dressing the wounds of the men as they were brought down, or in serving such as were thirsty with a drink of clean water. Some of them pretended, or were really so much affected by the shocking sight around them, that they were totally unable to render any assistance to the sufferers. Two of the number, I think it but justice to mention, acted with the greatest calmness and self possession.[52]

The surgeon's quarters were enough to turn anyone's stomach, as M'Pherson's description shows:

> Illuminated by the dim light of a few pursers' dips, the surgeon and assistants were busily employed in amputating, binding up, and attending to the different cases as they were brought to them. The stifled groans, the figures of the surgeon and his mates, their bare arms and faces smeared with blood, the dead and dying all round, some in the last agonies of death, and others screaming under the amputating knife, formed a horrid scene of misery, and made a hideous contrast to the "pomp, pride and circumstance of war."[53]

While criticizing the squeamishness of the women, M'Pherson admitted that he himself almost fainted when he visited the cockpit after the battle: "The heavy smell of the place, and the stifled groans of my suffering shipmates brought a cold sweat over me; and I found myself turn so sick that I was obliged to sit down for a little on one of the steps of the ladder."[54]

Women in the French Navy
Women also served in battle in the enemy's ships. At the Battle of Trafalgar, fought on 21 October 1805, two Frenchwomen were

M. Dubourg, colored aquatint after a drawing by William Heath. This romanticized view depicts the rescue of the Frenchwoman Jeannette by British seamen after her ship, the *Achille*, exploded and burned at the Battle of Trafalgar, 1805. NATIONAL MARITIME MUSEUM, GREENWICH, LONDON

pulled from the water by British boat crews after their ship, the seventy-four-gun *Achille*, exploded. The *Achille* had lost all her senior officers before she caught fire and blew up at sunset, by which time the fighting had almost ceased. The British rescued over two hundred of her company, but many drowned before the boats could pick them up. Over four hundred of the crew were lost in the battle.

One of the women, identified only by her first name, Jeannette, was originally from French Flanders. She had been stationed in the passage of the fore-magazine in the hold of the *Achille*, assisting in handing up the powder to the gun decks. When she realized that the ship was on fire, she scrambled up to the lower deck, climbed through a gunport, and leaped into the sea just before the ship exploded. She was burned on her neck and shoulders by molten lead falling around her, but she was able to cling to a plank for several hours until she was rescued by a British boat and taken to the *Revenge*, where she was given a cot in the officers' quarters. Three days after the battle, having no idea if her husband was still alive, she went to the section of the ship where the French seamen were held to seek word of him. There he was, safe and sound. The couple was sent ashore at Gibraltar, a long way from Jeannette's home in Flanders.[55]

The other woman from the *Achille* was taken on board the *Britannia*. She was naked when pulled from the water, having shed her clothing to keep from being pulled down by the wet garments. Second Lieutenant Halloran of the *Britannia's* marines recorded in his journal, "Our senior subaltern of marines, Lieutenant Jackson, gave her a large cotton dressing-gown for clothing." She too was sent to Gibraltar.[56]

More British Women in Battle

A newspaper at Mahon, on the island of Minorca, reported the sad story of the able seaman Joseph Phelan and his wife and baby on board the sloop *Swallow* in an engagement fought on 16 June 1812. Phelan, an Irishman, was twenty-four when he first entered the *Swallow* at Plymouth in April 1809.[57] Perhaps Mrs. Phelan came on board at that time. On the day of the battle she assisted the surgeon despite having given birth three weeks earlier to a son, Tommy. Tommy was probably placed somewhere in the cockpit among the wounded, not an ideal nursery, but in sight of his mother. As Mrs. Phelan was attending one of her husband's (and her own) wounded messmates, she heard that her husband had been hit. She rushed up to where he was lying on the main deck, and as she took him in her arms, a shot took her head off. He died immediately afterwards.

Following the battle, Phelan's messmates addressed the problem of the orphaned Tommy; he desperately needed nourishment. At first they had little hope that he could be saved, but then one of them thought of the Maltese goat that provided the officers with milk. The officers agreed to lend the goat to suckle the baby, and at the time the news report was written—10 July 1812, three weeks after the death of his parents—Tommy was still on board, being cared for by the seamen and nursed by the goat, and was thriving.[58]

One seaman's wife received a pension in her own right for having been wounded in the line of duty even though her name was not listed in the ship's muster book. Eleanor Moor petitioned for a pension from Chatham Chest for "a fracture of the cranium." She had received the wound on board H.M.S. *Apollo* in action with a French frigate on 15 June 1780 "while carrying powder to a gun at which her husband was quartered." The governors of Chatham Chest wrote to the lords of the Admiralty on 11 August 1780 asking for special approval of Eleanor Moor's request, "there being no precedent for the relief of persons not borne on the Ship's Books."[59] The lords approved the application the next day, a singularly generous decision; perhaps she was personally known to one of them. She was awarded an annual pension of four pounds, a meager but standard amount.[60]

A LONG TRADITION ENDS

The number of women in naval vessels at sea gradually decreased after 1815 during the relatively peaceful years that followed the close of hostilities with France, although a few warrant officers' wives continued to go to sea until midcentury. During the years 1839–43, for example, Mrs. Bull, the wife of the boatswain of the twenty-eight-gun *Rattlesnake,* sailed with her husband in the East Indies and China. He had served in the Napoleonic Wars and had probably been taking Mrs. Bull to sea for the past thirty years, and the captain, also a veteran of those wars, was accustomed to having warrant officers' wives in his ship.[61]

In the steamships of the later half of the nineteenth century, only commissioned officers' wives went to sea, and then only in carefully specified circumstances. By midcentury the navy was changing from its old ways whereby tradition had ruled and captains had run their ships as they saw fit.

In contrast to the earlier *Regulations and Instructions,* which simply stated that women should not be carried to sea without permission, the later *Queen's Regulations and Admiralty Instructions* gave detailed guidelines concerning women at sea, and commanding officers were expected to conform to the rules exactly as written. It is worth quoting these later orders in order to show just how scant the earlier ones had been. The following *Queen's Regulations* of 1879 are representative of those issued during the late nineteenth century:

> No wife of any Officer or Man, nor any other woman, is to be allowed to reside on board or to take passage in a Ship except upon the express authority of the Admiralty, or when time and circumstance do not admit of a reference home, of the Commander in Chief abroad.
>
> This authority may only be exercised by a Commander in Chief abroad when the ship is about to make a direct passage to one port from another and back; but on no account is it to be exercised when ships are cruising for practice or for evolutionary purposes; and every case is at, or before, embarkation to be specially reported to the Admiralty.
>
> Whenever a Senior Officer may, on the formal requisition of an Ambassador, Minister, Chargé d'Affaires or Consul or of the Governor or Lieutenant-Governor of a Colony, receive, or order to be received, any woman for passage, he will at once report the circumstance to his Commander in Charge for the information of the Admiralty.
>
> The Captain will in his Quarterly Return of Passengers [no such list was required under the earlier *Regulations*] be careful to include the name and particulars of every woman embarked or carried to sea during the quarter, except for the wives and daughters of Military persons embarked during the period [whose names would appear in army records].[62]

WOMEN DEPRIVED OF THE GENERAL SERVICE MEDAL

In 1847 it was decided that Queen Victoria would award a Naval General Service Medal to all the still living survivors of the major battles fought between 1793 and 1840—to all, that is, except the women.

Three women applied for the medal: Mary Ann Riley and Ann Hopping, who had participated in the Battle of the Nile in 1798, forty-nine years earlier, and Jane Townshend, who had served in the *Defiance* at Trafalgar in 1805. The four admirals who formed the committee to decide who would get the medal at first agreed to give it to women. Sir Thomas Byam Martin, the committee's spokesman, wrote regarding Jane Townshend's application, "The Queen in the *Gazette* of the first of June [1847] directs all who were *present* in this action shall have a medal, without any reservation as to sex, and as this woman produces from the captain of the *Defiance* strong and highly satisfactory certificates of her useful services during the action, she is fully entitled to a medal."[63]

Then, however, Admiral Martin went on to explain that the committee had had second thoughts. Someone, very likely the queen herself, had disapproved of their initial decision. The idea of a woman participating in a naval battle was distasteful to Victoria. The queen was strongly convinced that a woman should know her place, which was at home and under the control of a man. (She later bitterly opposed the campaign for women's rights. "God created men and women different," she said. "Let them remain each in their own position.")[64] Admiral Martin explained the committee's final decision to disallow women's claims to the medal: "Upon further consideration this [giving of the medal to women] cannot be allowed. There were many women in the fleet equally useful, and it will leave the Army exposed to *innumerable* applications of the same nature." The reasons given for denying the three women the medal were clearly nonsense. More than twenty thousand men received it, some simply because they had been on board during a battle. Daniel Tremendous McKenzie, for example, was presented with the medal for having been born in the *Tremendous* during the battle of the Glorious First of June, 1794. His rank is listed in the medal roll as "baby." His mother, if she was still alive in 1847, could not receive the medal.[65]

The four admirals on the committee, although not from a class known for its support of the rights of women, were honorable men who recognized that the women were entitled to the medal. However, they capitulated to political pressure. In the end, they decided to conform to the traditional government stance of centuries: women who went to sea on the lower deck of naval vessels officially did not exist.[66]

CHAPTER 3

Women in Disguise in Naval Crews

Oh, Pretty Susan left her home
And sailed away so far.
She braved the tempests, storms and gales,
Feared neither wound nor scar,
And done her duty manfully
On board a Man of War.

—"Susan's Adventures in a Man of War"

THERE ARE VERIFIED ACCOUNTS of more than twenty women who joined the Royal Navy or Marines dressed as men in the period from the late seventeenth to the early nineteenth century. Some of them served for years before their true gender was discovered. Undoubtedly there were others whose male disguise was never penetrated, and whose stories have therefore gone unrecorded.

I have chosen to refer to women in naval crews as *women seamen*—an odd usage, but more accurate than the term *women sailors,* since the word *sailors* covers all those who work in ships, whatever their rank. Furthermore, in the age of sail the term *sailors* was usually applied to the crews of merchant ships, while *seamen* was used for naval crews.

There are three major questions about women seamen:

1. How were they able to pass as male on board a crowded ship where there was no privacy?
2. Why did they volunteer for the navy or marines and go to great efforts to remain on board when many of the men had to be forced on board and deserted whenever they got the chance?
3. How were they viewed by their fellow seamen, by their officers, and by society as a whole once their true gender was revealed?

Before addressing these questions we need to look at a few accounts of these women in order to have a context in which to discuss them.

FOUR WOMEN SEAMEN

The Gentlewoman Anne Chamberlyne

One of the earliest known cases of a woman seaman is that of Anne Chamberlyne, who in 1690 joined her brother's ship and fought in the battle against the French off Beachy Head. Unlike most women seamen, who were of the lower classes, she came from the gentry. A tablet to her memory was placed in the wall of Chelsea Old Church (All Saints), Cheyne Walk, London, with other Chamberlyne family memorials. It was destroyed, together with that entire section of the church, during World War II, but a record of its Latin inscription has been preserved.[1] Here is a translation:

> In an adjoining vault lies Anne, the only daughter of Edward Chamberlyne, Doctor of Laws, born in London, the 20th January, 1667, who having long declined marriage [at age twenty-three], and aspiring to great achievements unusual to her sex and age, on the 30th June, 1690, on board a fireship in

man's clothing, as a second Pallas, chaste and fearless, fought valiantly six hours against the French, under the command of her brother....

Returned from the engagement, and after some few months married to John Spragg, Esq., with whom, for sixteen more [months], she lived most amiably happy. At length, in childbed of a daughter, she encountered death, 30th October 1691. This monument, for a consort most virtuous and dearly loved, was erected by her husband.

Snatched, alas, how soon by sudden death, unhonoured by a progeny like herself, worthy to rule the Main![2]

The Chamberlynes were a prosperous, scholarly, and somewhat eccentric family. Anne's father studied law at Oxford; his monument notes that "he had seven children and wrote six books." The books were coated with wax and buried with him. The brother whose ship Anne Chamberlyne joined, Captain Peregrine Clifford Chamberlyne, was not only an expert in navigation but also a linguist and doctor of law. Another brother, John, was gentleman of the privy chamber to both Queen Anne and George I, and among his published works were his translations of the Lord's Prayer into one hundred languages.[3]

A fellow parishioner of Anne Chamberlyne at Chelsea Old Church was Mrs. Mary Astell (1668–1731), a classics scholar and an early advocate of women's rights. She even attempted to found a college for women, a radical notion that was quickly quashed by her male colleagues. The two women were only one year apart in age, and in the same year that Anne Chamberlyne went to sea, Mary Astell published her essay "Defence of the Fair Sex."[4] In their respective searches for freedom from the strictures imposed on women of their day, they may well have influenced each other.

Another Gentlewoman

Another woman from the upper classes went to sea two years after Chamberlyne's service. The parliamentarian Narcissus Luttrell

noted in his diary on 19 November 1692, "A gentlewoman has petitioned the Queen, setting forth that the last summer she served in
man's clothes on board the *St. Andrew,* which was engaged in the
fight with the French, and producing a certificate thereof, [since]
she quitted herself well, she desired something to be given her."[5] It
is interesting that her petition was addressed not, as was usual, to
the king but to the queen. Perhaps she thought a woman would be
more sympathetic. There is no record of whether or not she ever
received her back pay.

The Woman Marine Known as William Prothero

A more typical example of the women who served in the ships of
the sailing navy is the marine known as William Prothero, who
served in 1760–61 in the appropriately named thirty-two-gun
Amazon, Captain Basil Keith. Her service is confirmed in three
sources: the captain's log, the ship's muster, and a personal journal.
In Prothero's case, as in many such cases, only her male alias is
recorded; her female name was considered to be irrelevant.

The entry in the captain's log for 20 April 1761 at Yarmouth was
brief: "One of the marines going by the name of Wm. Protherow
was discovered to be a woman. She had done her duty on board
nine months."[6]

The *Amazon*'s muster book records that Private William Prothero
entered 1 December 1760 and was discharged 30 April 1761. (This
record of her having served five months is probably more accurate
than the estimate of nine months' service given in the captain's log.
How much pay the men received was based on the data in the
muster book, and the navy did not fool around in matters of
money.) As is usual in such cases, the muster book avoids men-
tioning that Prothero was dismissed because she had been found
to be a woman. The reason for discharge is simply given as "per
Admiralty order."[7]

The third mention of Prothero is found in the journal of J. C.
Dickinson, a surgeon's mate in the *Amazon.* He described her as "an

eighteen-year-old Welsh girl who had followed her sweetheart to sea."[8] It is most unlikely that Prothero joined the marines for this reason; if her lover had been on board, she could simply have gone to sea with him as his woman. (We will return later to this dubious notion that women went to sea to find their lost lovers.)

The Woman Seaman Known as William Brown

During the Napoleonic Wars a black woman known as William Brown served in the navy for a dozen years, perhaps more. Once again, no one believed it important to record her real name. She joined the navy around 1804 and served at least until 1816, perhaps much longer. In September 1815 a London newspaper revealed the details of her naval career up to that time:

> Amongst the crew of the *Queen Charlotte,* 110 guns, recently paid off [31 August 1815], it is now discovered was a female African who had served as a seaman in the Royal Navy for upwards of eleven years, several of which she had been rated able on the books of the above ship, by the name of William Brown. [She] has served for some time as the captain of the foretop, highly to the satisfaction of the officers.[9]

The most experienced and dependable of the able seamen were appointed to be "captain" of a particular section of the ship—the foretop (the upper section of the foremast), the maintop (the mainmast), the forecastle, and so forth—to lead the other seamen assigned to that section. A captain of the topmen not only had to be agile and unafraid of heights; he had to be experienced in working the sails, both from the deck and aloft. He also needed to have gained the respect of his fellow seamen, who must follow his lead without hesitation. The topmen's job was extremely perilous, especially in stormy weather, when they had to take in sails high above the rolling deck in a roaring wind. Many a man fell to his death.

The news report about Brown continues:

> She is a smart, well-formed figure, about five feet four inches in
> height, possessed of considerable strength and great activity;
> her features are rather handsome for a black, and she appears
> to be about twenty-six years of age. Her share of prize money is
> said to be considerable, respecting which she has been several
> days at Somerset Place [in London where the Pay Office was
> located].
>
> In her manner she exhibits all the traits of a British tar and
> takes her grog with her late messmates with the greatest gaiety.
> She says she is a married woman and went to sea in consequence
> of a quarrel with her husband, who it is said has entered a caveat
> against her receiving her prize money. [A husband legally con-
> trolled his wife's earnings.]
>
> She declares her intention of again entering the service as a
> volunteer.[10]

Brown not only reentered the service on 31 December 1815 but
even rejoined her old ship, whose officers, surprisingly, were either
unaware of the news story or chose to ignore it.

The *Queen Charlotte's* muster book gives Brown's place of origin as Edinburgh, her rating as AB (able seaman), and her age as
thirty-two.[11] Upon her reentry she received two months' advance
wages and made the small purchase of 1s. 7d. worth of slop clothes,
and the very large purchase of 9s. 6d. worth of tobacco, an amount
equal to almost a fourth of her monthly wages.[12] (Many women
seamen smoked or chewed tobacco, perhaps in an effort to appear
manly.) In January 1816 Brown was appointed, not captain of the
foretop, but captain of the forecastle, a less physically demanding
job.[13] Forecastle men were usually older and less sprightly than the
men assigned to the masts.

It is unusual to find a woman in a naval crew as old as Brown;
it was much more difficult for an older woman to pass as a man
than it was for a young woman to pass as a boy. In the latter case

the woman's lack of whiskers could be explained by her youth. Brown apparently looked young for her age; recall that the 1815 news report put her age at twenty-six when she was in fact thirty-two. Perhaps being black also helped her to pass, since black men are often less hirsute than white men. She was also aided in maintaining her male role by the fact that she had been in the navy since she was twenty-one, and over the years her messmates had come to accept her as one of them.

On 29 June 1816 Brown, together with some other seamen, was transferred from the *Queen Charlotte* into the *Bombay*, and at that point we lose track of her, since there is no extant muster for the *Bombay* for that period.[14]

How Women Seamen Passed as Men

It was not difficult for a young woman in male dress to join the navy or marines in the eighteenth and early nineteenth centuries, a period when England was almost continuously at war and the navy was usually desperately short of crews. Officers were not apt to inquire too closely into the background of a healthy young volunteer at a time when they were driven to accept almost any poor wretch whom the press gangs could grab, including the old, the sick, and the criminal. A typical complaint about the quality of recruits is expressed in a letter to the Admiralty written by Admiral Philip Cavendish, commander at Portsmouth, in July 1739:

> The 524 men that were sent from the Nore in the *Burford* and *Pearl,* to man Mr. Vernon's squadron, are distributed on board them, but surely there never was such wretches, many of them boys of fourteen or fifteen years of age,…and some upwards of sixty or seventy; but that is not the worst, for I believe there are above one hundred of them that must be turned away, being bursten, full of the pox, itch, lame, king's evil, and all other distempers, from the hospitals at London, and will serve only to breed an infection in the ships; for the rest, most of them are

thieves, housebreakers, Newgate birds [inmates of Newgate, a London prison], and the very filth of London.[15]

It is difficult for us today to appreciate how casually recruits were accepted into the navy. There was seldom any physical examination upon entry, nor was proof of identity required. Neither volunteers nor impressed men were "sworn in" or "signed on"; many were illiterate and unable to sign their names. They were simply lined up on deck, and a lieutenant listed each man in the muster book, writing down whatever name was given, spelled as he chose.[16]

Once a woman had taken her place among the crew on the lower deck of her ship, there was no routine situation in which she was required to undress. Seamen seldom bathed, and they slept in their day clothes. It was only when a seaman was flogged that he was ordered to be stripped to the waist, and it was in this situation that several seamen were discovered to be women.

Even when a man was sick or wounded, he received only the most cursory examination; only the afflicted part of the body was examined. The marine Hannah Snell spent many months in a government-run hospital in Cuddalore, India, in 1748–49, and the doctors treated wounds in both her thighs without ever realizing that she was a woman.[17]

Reports of women seamen do not tell how they managed to deal with urination and menstruation, but it was not as difficult as it might seem. To urinate a woman could go to the "head" (the toilet facilities at the bow of the ship overhanging the water) when no one else was there. Several accounts of women in male disguise in the army report that they attached a short tube to their underclothing to use in urinating, but a woman seaman would find such a device difficult to use in rough weather.

The very fact that a ship was so crowded, and crowded with such a motley collection of people having various physical complaints, meant that the men tended to keep a psychological distance from one another. Their philosophy was to live and let live. They ignored, if they could, any strange behavior or evidence of sickness in their mates. Such circumstances aided a woman in hiding her menstrual periods. If someone noticed that a woman seaman was menstruating, he probably assumed that she was suffering from venereal disease, a common complaint of seamen. It is also possible that in some cases a woman's periods stopped because of the bad diet and strenuous physical activity on board.

In several cases, after a woman seaman's secret was discovered, she was sexually harassed. In the 1690s the seaman John Curtin wrote about the attempted seduction of a woman in disguise in his ship, the *Edgar,* a third-rate vessel of seventy-two guns, commanded by Captain Andrew Pedder. Curtin's account is in the form of a crudely constructed ballad:

VERSE 2

This Maiden she was press'd, Sir,
    and so was many more,
And she, among the rest, Sir,
    was brought down to the Nore,
Where ev'ry one did think they had
Prest a very pretty colliers lad;
    but yet it prov'd not so,
    when they the truth did know,
    they search'd her well below,
    and see how things did go,
    and found her so and so,
And then swore, the like was never known before.

VERSE 3

But at length a sailor bold, Sir,
    that us'd to sport and play, Sir.

Did chance for to behold, Sir,
   where this young Damsel lay, Sir,
Who thought she like a Maid did speak,
When he felt, she did begin to squeak,
   by which he found that she
   could not a sailor be,
   he strove to feel her knee,
   but she would not agree,
   but strove from him to flee,
And he said that she was certainly a Maid.[18]

A similar case in a privateer was reported in a Liverpool newspaper on 20 May 1757:

> A young person, five feet high, aged about nineteen, who entered in January last on board the *Resolution* privateer, Captain Barber, under the name of Arthur Douglas, proceeded with the ship from London to this port. [She] was, on Saturday last, discovered to be a woman by one of her messmates.... [To keep him from revealing her secret] she then promised to permit him to keep her company when they arrived there [in Liverpool]; but as soon as they came into port [she] refused his addresses.[19]

It appears that her rejected suitor then, out of spite, told the authorities about her.

A woman passing as male in a French naval expedition to the Pacific was sexually harassed by seamen after her true gender was discovered. In Louis Antoine de Bougainville's circumnavigation (1766–69), Jeanne Baré, under the name of Jean Baré, acted as male servant and assistant to the expedition's botanist, Philibert Commerson. She served without incident until, a year away from France, she was recognized as a woman by the natives of Tahiti as soon as she stepped ashore. After that, Bougainville reported, "it was difficult to prevent the sailors from alarming her modesty."[20]

WHY WOMEN JOINED THE NAVY OR MARINES

A prime reason why a woman joined the navy or marines was to escape the restricted economic and social status assigned to women. It was, however, only the most daring and unconventional woman who was willing to take the extraordinary step of changing her gender role in order to gain the social and financial advantages of a man. While the life of a male seaman was generally more restricted than that of a man of the same class in civilian life, a woman seaman found social freedom in the navy that she could not find on shore. On land she was banned from most profitable jobs and from many recreational and social activities. On shipboard a woman seaman was able to join the men as an equal in both work and play. She was no longer treated with condescension by her male peers.

Unlike most male recruits, a woman who joined the navy or marines usually improved her financial status. Although naval pay was low and slow in coming, when it did arrive a woman seaman could at least spend it as she chose; on land a woman was seldom in control of her own money. There was also the possibility of learning a trade not open to women. Mary Lacy, who served in the navy as William Chandler from 1759 to 1771, rose from carpenter's servant to fully qualified shipwright. (See chapter 4.)[21]

In several cases economic need was the reason why a woman joined the navy or marines. In 1807 Elizabeth Bowden, a fourteen-year-old orphan, finding herself alone and destitute in the naval port of Plymouth, put on boy's clothes and joined the navy.[22]

Jane Meace tried to join the marines in order to get the bounty money given to volunteers. Her case was reported in *Lloyd's Evening Post and British Chronicle* for 1 December 1762:

UTTOXETER, NOVEMBER 25: On Thursday, the twelfth instant, in the evening, a young girl in men's clothes, came to a recruiting party of marines at the Plume of Feathers and enlisted. [Recruiting sessions were usually held at a tavern, with posters distributed in advance advertising the date and place of rendezvous and offering a bounty to volunteers.] She wanted the whole bounty money in hand, being in want of clothing and other necessaries, but they would give her only one shilling till morning, but had the bowl of punch in and the point of war beat. The party [of recruits] lay that night in one bed with her [two or three per bed was the usual accommodation at an inn], and in the morning, one of the men laying hold of her coat over the breast to see how it fitted, her sex was discovered. She enlisted by the name of John Meace, but her proper name is Jane Meace, and [she] is well known in this country.[23]

A woman seaman had one great advantage over her male ship-mates: she could gain her discharge at any time simply by reveal-ing her true gender. When, in the words of contemporary reports, "her sex was discovered," she was not even chastised, let alone pros-ecuted. She was simply discharged "per Admiralty order." Few women seamen and marines, however, took this option. While the men deserted whenever they could, in almost every case a woman seaman, despite the hard work and bad living conditions, remained in the service until her gender was discovered and she was forced to leave.

The Restricted Role of Women in Society
In order to realize the extent of the advantages a woman gained in adopting a male identity, it is necessary to review the restrictions that society placed upon women. During the eighteenth and early nineteenth centuries, women, whatever their class, were usually constrained within a domestic setting, either in their own homes or as servants in the household of a more affluent family.

A single woman's money, if she had any, was controlled by her father or brother, or even her employer, especially if she was in domestic service, as most employed women were. Education was primarily restricted to men, except for training in the domestic arts.

Women were barred from most trades, they were consistently given the lowest-paying jobs, and they were paid less money than men doing the same work.

It was assumed that every young woman's goal was marriage; spinsters were viewed as failures. Nevertheless, a single woman had more control over her life than a married one. William Blackstone, the eighteenth-century legal authority, summarized the status of a married woman: "By marriage," he said, "the husband and wife are one person in law; that is, the very being or legal existence of the woman is suspended during the marriage."[24] A married woman owned nothing; all her assets, including her earnings and the personal property she brought to the marriage—even her jewelry and her clothing—were vested in her husband, who could spend or sell her belongings as he chose. By law a wife had to obey her husband, and if she did not, her husband could beat her into submission.

A man could actually sell his wife to another man. Over two hundred authenticated cases were recorded in England between 1760 and 1880.[25] Wife-selling was a substitute for divorce in a period when divorce was almost impossible for a lower-class man to obtain, and entirely beyond the reach of women. A wife sale was carried out in a traditional way: the wife, with a halter around her neck, was sold at auction at a market or inn or other public place where the event could be publicly witnessed.[26] Newspaper reports of these sales usually treated them as a joke. The following example is representative:

> ELEVEN OF MARCH, 1766. One Higginson, a journeyman carpenter, having last week sold his wife to a brother workman in a fit of conjugal indifference at the alehouse, took it into his head to hang himself a few days after, as the lady very peaceably cohabited with the purchaser, and refused to return home at his [her husband's] most pressing solicitations.[27]

It was beyond the imagination of most eighteenth-century men to think of a woman as a responsible adult, capable of managing her own life. One of the few Englishmen to address the subject of the subjugated status of women was the physician William Alexander, who gave a lucid analysis of their situation in his book *The History of Women,* published in 1782. He wrote:

> In Britain, we allow a woman to sway our sceptre, but by law and custom we debar her from every other government but that of her own family, as if there were not a public employment between that of superintending the kingdom and the affairs of her own kitchen which could be managed by the genius and capacity of woman. We neither allow women to officiate at our altars, to debate in our councils, nor to fight for us in the field; we suffer them not to be members of our senate, to practice any of the learned professions, nor to concern themselves much with our trades and occupations.
>
> We exercise nearly a perpetual guardianship over them, both in their virgin and their married state; and she who, having laid a husband in the grave, enjoys an independent fortune, is almost the only woman among us who can be called free.[28]

Women Seamen Identified with Men
In view of the low status accorded them, it is not surprising that a few ambitious young women took on the male role. It took more than poverty and ambition, however, to provoke a woman to reject the role assigned to her by her culture. Cultural strictures are very strong; not many women in any society take the drastic step of acquiring a male identity in order to gain release from the prohibitions imposed on them.

The women who joined naval crews were a very small minority who, because of their special physical and emotional traits, were willing and able to adopt a male role. They were strong and athletic enough to perform the work assigned them: to clamber up the rigging and to take in sail in heavy weather, to pull heavy lines and to take their place among the men at the capstan heaving up the anchor. They joined in the rough games and tough badinage of their shipmates; they chewed tobacco, downed their grog, and acquired the rolling gait and the bellowing voice of the sailor. Indeed, a compelling reason why most of these women joined naval crews was their strong desire to adopt the sexual aspects of a man. Their transvestism was not just a means to an end; they enjoyed cross-dressing. Many if not most women seamen and marines physically and emotionally identified with men; they felt comfortable passing as male.

It was difficult for a woman to change her gender role in her own community where she was known, and equally difficult to switch her gender and then find work in a new place where she had no contacts or references. The navy or marines offered an opportunity for her to take on the role of a man in a setting where she was not known and where no proof of identity or previous experience was needed.

Once a woman had established a male identity in the navy, she usually continued to pass as a man when she returned to civilian life. In 1761, for example, a press gang in Plymouth picked up a woman dressed in men's clothes who had previously served almost five years as a marine. She revealed her true gender only after she was confined in a prison cell to await assignment to a ship and became claustrophobic. She gave her name as Hannah Witney and said she was born in Ireland, "and would not have disclosed herself if she had been allowed her liberty."[29]

Another case of a woman seaman who kept her male identity on shore was reported in the *Naval Chronicle* of 1807:

At the Public Office, Queen Square [London], an old woman, generally known by the name of Tom Bowling, was lately brought before the magistrate for sleeping all night in the street and was committed as a rogue and vagabond and passed to her parish. She served as boatswain's mate on board a man-of-war for upwards of twenty years and has a pension from Chatham Chest. When waked at midnight by the watchman in the street, covered with snow, she cried, "Where the devil would you have me sleep?" She has generally slept in this way, and dresses like a man; and is so hardy at a very advanced age that she never catches cold.[30]

Some women seamen sought women as sexual partners. When Hannah Snell's ship, the *Eltham,* was returning to England from India in 1750 and the crew were given shore leave at Lisbon, Snell, under the name of James Gray, and her fellow marine Edward Jefferies frequently went on shore "in quest of adventures":

> Amongst other frolics these two cronies pursued an amour together by contracting an acquaintance with two young women of the place that had no nun's flesh about them. When they [Gray and Jefferies] set sail for England, the enamoured women would fain have quitted their native place to have had the plea-sure of a voyage with their sweethearts, but the captain had given express orders that no women should be admitted on board on any pretense how plausible soever.[31]

Mary Lacy was candid about her own pursuit of various women. In the preface to her autobiography, however, where she explains her "motives for endeavouring to be as frequently as possible in the company of women in the way of courtship," she offers the ridicu-lous disclaimer that she sought out women in order "to avoid the conversation of the men," which was "very offensive to a delicate ear."[32]

Although it is evident that many women seamen enjoyed the role of the randy sailor, their chroniclers were careful to assure readers that in the final analysis these women were "normal" het-erosexuals who had joined up for socially acceptable motives.

One acceptable motive was patriotism. The seaman-balladeer John Curtin tacked a patriotic motive onto the story of the *Edgar*'s woman seaman. Although at the beginning of the ballad he noted that the woman was forced on board the *Edgar* by a press gang, in his closing verses he said that, after learning that her lover had joined the army to fight for his king, she decided in a burst of patriotic fer-vor "to go to sea so that she might serve the King as well as he."[33]

The Lost-Lover Theme

By far the most frequently given reason for a woman enlisting in
the navy or marines, and the most patently absurd, was that she was
seeking her male lover who had either run off to sea or been forced
on board a ship by a press gang. This ubiquitous motif, which I call
the lost-lover theme, is found wherever women seamen are mentioned. It was a popular theme of British ballads from the sixteenth
century into the twentieth; variations were still being sung in the
1930s, not only in Great Britain but also in seafaring communities
in Labrador and Nova Scotia.[34]

The earliest example that I have found of a "lost-lover ballad"
is "The Marchants Daughter of Bristow," first printed in the 1590s.
The basic elements of its plot were repeated in numerous later ballads. When Maudlin, the merchant's daughter, falls in love with a
young man, her family and friends reject him as a social inferior,
and her father forces him to break off the relationship and to leave
England. The night before his departure he comes to Maudlin's
window and, in a serenade, bids her farewell. "In tears she spends
the doleful night, wishing herself (though naked) with her faithful friend," but by morning her tears are dry, and she has concocted a plan to dress in "ship-boy's garments" and to follow her lover
to sea. After many adventures at sea and on land, Maudlin finds
him in Italy, and the happy couple return to England, inherit her
father's money, and live happily ever after.[35]

While in many later ballads the lovelorn woman is not a rich
man's daughter, she always goes to sea in male disguise in order to
join her sweetheart, and she is always pretty and frail, with delicate lily-white hands. In contrast, the young women who actually
joined the navy cannot have been so very fragile. On the contrary,
they must have had the build and demeanor of a sturdy boy, or they
would not have succeeded in their male impersonation.

A representative example of these ballads is "Young Henry of the
Raging Main":

Woodcut from the broadside ballad "Young Henry of the Raging Main." The ballad tells of a young woman, Emma, who, disguised as a man, goes to sea with her lover, Henry. Is this jaunty figure male or female? In either case, it is a naive rendering by a landlubber: no one would have been allowed to smoke near a gun, where loose gunpowder could ignite. From John Ashton, ed., *Modern Street Ballads* (London: Chatto and Windus, 1888), 253. BOSTON ATHENAEUM

VERSE 4

Cried Henry, "Love, don't be distracted,
  Perhaps you may be cast away."
"Tis for that reason," cried young Emma,
  "That behind I will not stay.
I'll dress myself in man's apparel,
  So, dearest Henry, don't complain,
In jacket blue, and tarry trousers,
  I will plough the raging main."

VERSE 5

Then on board the brig Eliza,
  Henry and his Emma went;
She did her duty like a sailor,
  And with her lover was content.
Her pretty hands, once soft as velvet,
  With pitch and tar appeared in pain,
Though her hands were soft, she went aloft,
  And boldly ploughed the raging main.[36]

This broadside ballad is probably based on an actual case of a woman seaman who served in the brig *Eliza*. Broadside ballads—single sheets of crudely printed text, usually illustrated with a woodcut—were hawked on city streets for as little as a farthing each (a quarter of a penny). The poorer classes who could not afford newspapers, which cost a penny or more, got much of their news from ballad sheets. Some ballads related traditional folklore; others covered current events such as naval victories or public hangings. There was no attempt made to distinguish fact from fiction.

The lost-lover theme became so embedded in the folk tradition of the culture that when an actual case of a woman seaman was reported, the theme was often tacked on. In fact, one woman used it herself, apparently to avoid discussing very different motives. The *Annual Register* of 1771 reported:

A person by the name of Charles Waddall, of the *Oxford* man-of-war lying at Chatham, was ordered to receive two dozen lash-es for desertion; but when tied up to the gangway the culprit was discovered to be a woman. She declares that she has traveled from Hull to London after a man with whom she was in love, and hearing he was on board the *Oxford* at Chatham, she entered at the rendezvous in London for the same ship the ninth instant. On the seventeenth of this month she came on board, but finding that her sweetheart was run away, in consequence thereof, she deserted yesterday.

[Upon being discovered to be a woman,] she was immedi-ately carried before Admiral Dennis, who made her a present of half a guinea; Commissioner Hanway [the commissioner of Chatham Dockyard] and most of the officers of the yard made her presents also.[37]

She did not explain why she continued to maintain her male role after she learned that her lover was not on board, even when she was ordered to be flogged. The story is murky.

There is much about the lost-lover theme that is pure nonsense. Most sailor's sweethearts came from seafaring communities and would have known that a woman could usually go to sea with her lover in her own right; there was no need to adopt male disguise and join the crew. They would also have known that if a woman did join up, even if she were assigned to her lover's ship she might be transferred to another vessel at any time.

Unlikely as it was that a woman seaman had gone to sea to be with her lover, readers expected accounts of these women to include the lost-lover theme; it reassured them that the heroine was hetero-sexual even though it was added to the story in such a clumsy way that it was hard to believe.

A good example is found in the 1750 biography of the marine Hannah Snell. At about the age of twenty, while living in the sailor's town of Wapping on the outskirts of London, she is supposed to have married one James Summs, a Dutch sailor who deserted her when she was seven months pregnant. Conveniently for the plot of the story, the baby died at the age of seven months. Snell then put on male clothes and set off to find her husband and seek revenge. She did not, however, look for him among the ships nearby but set off overland on foot for distant land-bound Coventry, where under the name of James Gray she joined the army.[38] Official records confirm that Snell did live in Wapping and did join the army in Coventry, but it is unlikely that she ever had a husband named Summs or gave birth to his baby.

Further Confusions of Fact with Fiction

There are three eighteenth-century biographies of women who claimed to have gone to sea in ships of the Royal Navy: the biographies of Hannah Snell and Mary Anne Talbot have always been, and still are, accepted as the prime sources of information about English women seamen and marines, but Mary Lacy's autobiography, after an initial success, has been forgotten. This is unfortunate, for Snell's biography is packed with fictional embellishments, and Talbot never went to sea. Only Lacy's book, discussed in chapter 4, is a reliable source.

The Muddled Biography of Hannah Snell

Hannah Snell, who could read a little but could not write, dictated her story to a literary hack hired by the newspaper publisher Robert Walker, or perhaps to Walker himself, in 1750, soon after she returned from her stint in India with the marines. She was quite a celebrity at that time, and so he rushed two versions of her biography into print, one of 46 pages and the other of 187 pages. Unfortunately, the biography's author could not leave well enough alone; he turned Snell's remarkable adventures into a pretentious literary exercise, full of extraneous fictional material and flowery classical references. The many later accounts of Snell's story picked up the fiction along with the facts.[39] I have checked ships' muster

The marine Hannah Snell in civilian male clothing.
From *The Female Soldier; or, the Surprising Life and
Adventures of Hannah Snell* (London: R. Walker, 1750),
reproduced in Menie Muriel Dowie, ed., *Women
Adventurers* (London: T. Fisher Unwin, 1893), facing 55.
BOSTON ATHENAEUM

books and pension records in order to extricate the actual events from the welter of misinformation, and the following facts emerge.

Snell was born in Worcester in 1723, the daughter of a cloth dyer and hosier. At the age of twenty, after the death of both her parents, she went to live with her sister and brother-in-law, Susannah and James Gray, at their house in Wapping. After several years with them, for reasons we do not know, she borrowed her brother-in-law's clothes as well as his name, and on 27 November 1745 she joined Colonel John Guise's Sixth Regiment of Foot (Royal First Warwickshire) at Coventry, not far from her birthplace, and served in the army for a period somewhere between four months and two years. She then deserted.[40] Apparently she continued to go by the name of James Gray, and at Portsmouth in 1747 she enlisted under that name in Colonel Fraser's Regiment of Marines and was sent to the sloop *Swallow*, Captain John Rowsier. Soon after she went on board, the *Swallow* sailed for the east coast of India in Admiral Edward Boscawen's fleet.[41]

According to the muster book of the *Swallow*, the fleet reached "Cudalowe" (Cuddalore), India, in August 1748, and Snell and the other marines on board were sent on shore to join the long and unsuccessful siege of the French fortifications at Pondicherry. Snell was in the thick of the battle, which continued for several weeks, and she was severely wounded in both thighs. She was sent to the hospital at Cuddalore, where she remained for almost a year, and throughout this period the doctors who treated her never discovered that she was a woman. There may not be any truth in the biographer's claim that in order to avoid discovery, she herself removed shot from her groin with the help of an Indian nurse; but there is no doubt that she was determined to keep her male status.[42] She was released on 2 August 1749 into the pink *Tartar*, where she served as a seaman while waiting to be assigned to a larger vessel, a not unusual procedure.[43]

Engraving, "The English Heroine or the British Amazon:
Hannah Snell . . . Drawn from ye Life, July 4th, 1750."
ROYAL MARINES MUSEUM, SOUTHSEA, HAMPSHIRE

On 13 October 1749 Snell was transferred from the *Tartar* to the *Eltham,* and in that ship she returned to Portsmouth. The *Eltham* reached Spithead on 25 May 1750 and was paid off. At this point Snell revealed her true identity and was discharged "per order of Admiral Hawke."[44]

According to the biography, upon returning to civilian life Snell continued to dress as a man, "having bought new clothing for that purpose."[45] The press got hold of her story—probably from Snell herself—and she became a celebrity. The two versions of her biography were bestsellers, she sat for several portraits, and she received a lot of press coverage, including a report in doggerel:

> *Hannah in briggs [breeches] behaved so well*
> *   That none her softer sex could tell;*
> *Nor was her policy confounded*
> *   When near the mark of nature wounded [shot in the groin].*
> . . . .
> *Oh, how her bedmate bit his lips,*
> *   And marked the spreading of her hips,*
> *And cursed the blindness of his youth*
> *   When she confessed the naked truth!*[46]

Her popularity was so great that she decided to go on the stage, and she worked at several London theaters, including the New Wells in Clerkenwell, where she joined tumblers and tightrope walkers in entertaining audiences as large as seven hundred. Dressed as a marine, she sang a ditty telling how she "ventured on the main, facing death and every danger, love and glory to obtain." She then led a group of young actresses, also in marine uniform, in a series of regimental marches.[47] The audiences loved her.

Eventually, however, Snell's popularity dimmed, and she left the stage and lived on a pension provided by Chelsea Hospital, the London hospital for army pensioners. This was for her service in both the army and the marines. (The marines were under army jurisdiction until 1747.) The entry in the admission book for 21 November 1750 reads, "2nd Mar. [Marines] ffrazer's [regiment], Hannah Snell, age 27. Time of service 4 1/2 months in this & Guise's Regt." (The length of service is wrong; Snell served in the marines from 1747 to 1750, a period of over two years.) "Wounded at Pondicherry in the thigh of both leggs, born at Worcester, her father a Dyer."[48]

The biography suggests that Snell planned to open a sailor's tavern in Wapping called the Woman in Masquerade, but it is doubtful that she had the money to do so; I could find no license for a tavern of that name nor an owner named James Gray or Hannah Snell anywhere in the London districts along the Thames.[49] It appears that at some point she left London and reverted to living as a woman. Newspapers reported in 1759 that she married Samuel Eyles, a carpenter, at Newbury, Berks County, and had a son by that marriage. According to one news report, she lived for a time with her son in Stoke Newington, a village that is today part of London. It was reported in 1772 that at age forty-nine, following the death of her first husband—or her second, if you believe that she had earlier married the Dutch sailor—she married Richard Habgood of Welford, Berks.

Snell's life ended tragically. In the 1780s she was judged insane and committed to Bethlehem Hospital—popularly known as Bedlam—in London. She died there on 8 February 1792 at the age of sixty-nine.[50]

The Spurious Autobiography of Mary Anne Talbot

Since its first publication in 1804, the so-called autobiography of Mary Anne Talbot (1778–1808) has been cited as a historical source in almost every work that touches on the subject of female sailors. Talbot was a well-known character in London in the early years of the nineteenth century, but her claim to have served in the navy and in French and American merchant ships was fabricated. Her story is embellished with the names of actual vessels and their captains, and in most instances official documents confirm that these ships were where the autobiography says they were. But in no case was there a seaman on board who could have been Talbot.

The earliest report of Talbot's alleged sea adventures appeared in the *Times* (London) of 4 November 1799. It is an interview at Middlesex Hospital "with a young and delicate female who calls herself Miss T——lb——t."[51] (It would be interesting to know why the *Times* suggested that Talbot was not her real name.) She told the news reporter that she was being treated for a shattered knee, which she claimed was an unhealed battle wound. She also gave the *Times* reporter a list of battles she claimed to have fought in that are completely different from her later claims. The *Times* reported that she had followed her lover, a naval officer, to sea.

Talbot's "autobiography" was published in 1804 in *Kirby's Wonderful and Scientific Museum; or, Magazine of Remarkable and Eccentric Characters,* a compendium of anecdotes and biographies, including that of Hannah Snell. (The Kirby version differs in many respects from the *Times* interview and does not include the lost-lover theme.)[52] Talbot's story proved so popular that Kirby printed an extended version in a separate volume in 1809, a year after her death, under the title *The Life and Surprising Adventures of Mary Anne Talbot in the Name of John Taylor, a Natural Daughter of the Late Earl Talbot...Related by Herself.*[53] Most later accounts were taken from this book.[54]

The autobiography was written by a literary hack hired by Robert Kirby, or perhaps by Kirby himself. Talbot was working for Kirby as a domestic servant when he first published her story, and she may have dictated some of it to him or his hireling. Although the book claims that Talbot spent nine years at an upper-class girls' boarding school, it is doubtful that she was more than barely literate. The autobiography follows the literary convention of the day whereby the heroine must be descended from at least the gentry and, if possible, from the aristocracy. Talbot claims, "I am the youngest of sixteen natural children whom my mother had by Lord William Talbot, Baron of Hensol."[55] This is extravagantly unlikely. What is known of Talbot's life in London shows her to have been of the underclass.

To give an idea of how fact and fiction are mixed in the 1809 autobiography, here are a few of the details. The evidence that proves the material to be fiction is given in parentheses.

According to the autobiography, Talbot was born in London in 1778. Her mother died at her birth, and for most of her childhood years she was placed under the control of a series of legal guardians. In January 1792, when she was fourteen, Talbot was passed along to army captain Essex Bowen "of the Eighty-second Regiment of Foot," who seduced her. "Intimidated by his manners," she says, "and knowing that I had no friend near me, I became everything he could desire."[56] Later that year, when Captain Bowen was ordered to the West Indies, he dressed her as a boy and took her along as his servant under the name of John Taylor. (There is no officer named Essex Bowen in the army lists of 1791–96, but strangely enough there is a Lieutenant Essex Bowen in the navy lists.[57] Perhaps Talbot's biographer ran across this officer's name when he was checking on naval reports from which to cull ships' names. The Eighty-second Regiment was not in existence in 1792 and was not sent to the West Indies until 1795, three years after Talbot claimed to have gone there with the regiment. Furthermore, the *Crown* transport in which Bowen and Talbot were supposed to have sailed to the West Indies did exist, but in 1792 that vessel was on her way back to England from India.[58])

Next the autobiography reports that Bowen, still with Talbot in tow, was sent to Europe. They both fought at Valenciennes (23 May–8 July 1793), and Bowen was killed. Talbot then deserted from the army, walked to Luxembourg, and there joined the crew of a French privateer that was soon captured by the English. Still using the name John Taylor, she was taken into the crew of the seventy-four-gun *Brunswick* and was wounded in the battle of the Glorious

First of June, 1794. (There is no John Taylor listed in the muster book of the *Brunswick* in 1794 who could be Talbot.)[59] When the *Brunswick* returned to Spithead, Talbot was sent to Haslar Naval Hospital in Gosport. (The name John Taylor is not among those sent from the *Brunswick* to Haslar, nor does the name appear in the hospital muster.)[60]

Adventure quickly follows adventure. Leaving Haslar, Talbot was assigned to the bomb *Vesuvius,* Captain Tomlinson, and soon after she went on board, the vessel was captured by the French in the English Channel. She then languished in a French prison for several years. (The *Vesuvius* was in the West Indies at this time and was not captured by the French.)[61] After her release Talbot served first as steward and then as mate of the schooner *Ariel,* an American merchant vessel out of New York; she stayed with the captain's family on shore and was courted by the captain's niece.[62] Finally, having returned to London, she was picked up by a press gang, and rather than spend more time in the navy, she revealed her gender. She was eighteen. So ends Talbot's tale of her life at sea.

The autobiography then describes Talbot's dissolute life in London where she frequented sailor's taverns in male dress, worked at various occupations including that of actress, suffered chronically from an injured leg, multiplied her debts, and established an intimate long-term relationship with a woman who even stayed with her in debtors' prison and supported her by doing needlework. Mary Anne Talbot died of general debility on 4 February 1808 at the age of thirty.

According to the autobiography, Talbot became such a celebrity in London that another woman tried to pass herself off as Mary Anne Talbot, but the "real Talbot" exposed her as a fraud.[63] This is an odd twist to the story, considering that Talbot herself was not what she claimed to be. The most surprising thing about the *Life and Surprising Adventures of Mary Anne Talbot* is that it has for so long been accepted as a historical account.

SOCIETY'S ATTITUDE TOWARD WOMEN SEAMEN AND MARINES

When a seaman or marine was discovered to be a woman, she was not reprimanded, let alone convicted and punished for having duped the navy by enlisting under a false identity. On the contrary, she suddenly gained the kindly attention of her officers. Previous to the revelation of her gender, when she was merely one of hundreds of seamen, she was below the notice of her ship's commissioned officers unless she misbehaved, in which case she was severely disciplined. But as soon as it was discovered that she was a woman, the officers' attitude toward her changed; they were fascinated by her and treated her with gentle solicitude, and often she was lauded in the press for her bravery and patriotism.

We have already noted the case of the woman seaman Charles Waddall, who was convicted of the very serious offense of desertion and ordered to be flogged.[64] As soon as it was realized that she was a woman, her punishment was canceled, and the most exalted of her superiors, including the admiral and the commissioner of Chatham Dockyard, rallied around to help her. They even gave her money from their own pockets.

A similar case was that of seventeen-year-old Margaret Thompson, who entered the navy under the name of George Thompson at Deptford in 1781.[65] A theft was committed on board her ship, a general search was made, and when women's apparel was found in Thompson's sea chest, the officer on duty assumed that she had stolen the clothes when last on shore. She was brought before the captain, who ordered that she should receive three dozen lashes. At this point she revealed that she was a woman.

The romantic, breathless style of the news report about Thompson is representative of such accounts: "Judge what astonishment pervaded the mind of everyone on board who little expected to find in the person of George Thompson a blooming youthful girl.... The resolution with which she performed the most arduous tasks, mounting aloft with amazing intrepidity in the midst of danger, even when the most experienced seamen appeared daunted, astonished everyone." Although the public were entranced by the vision of a "blooming girl" dressed as a man scampering up the rigging, they wanted to be reassured that there was no sexual deviation from accepted standards. This reassurance was, as usual, provided in the form of the lost-lover theme: "Being questioned by the Captain who she was and what could have induced her to take so extraordinary a step, she replied her name was Margaret Thompson, she had left her uncle, who lives in Northumberland Street [London], to see her sweetheart, who quitted England three years since, and is now resident at Bombay."[66]

The Long-Held Tolerance of Female Transvestites

To discuss society's attitude toward women seamen is primarily to discuss society's attitude toward female transvestites. Whenever a seaman was discovered to be a woman, it was not her sea adventures that people wanted to hear about; it was why she had adopted a male role.

Attitudes toward female transvestites in the eighteenth and nineteenth centuries were complex. The public liked to toy with the idea of a woman pretending to be a man, but she was not taken seriously; her cross-dressing was not viewed as a serious attempt to compete with men on any level—economic, social, or sexual. The public enjoyed hearing about a woman who had taken on a male role, but they liked to be reassured that she eventually reverted to her true gender. An account in the *Annual Register* for 1782 makes a point of noting that a former seaman emerged as an "elegant woman" as soon as she could afford to do so: "In September last, at Poplar [London], Mrs. Coles, who during the last war served on board several men-of-war as a sailor, after her discharge, upon a small fortune devolving to her, resumed the female character and was from that time considered as a very polite and elegant woman."[67]

Women passing as men were viewed very differently from the way transvestite men were judged. A man dressed in women's clothes was a threat to men in general; he lowered the dignity and prestige associated with maleness. A woman passing as a man did not undermine the superior position of men; she was dismissed as an inferior imitating a superior. Far from being intimidating to men, she was merely amusing, just as a child dressing up as an adult is amusing.

Moral standards in eighteenth-century England were greatly influenced by Christian doctrine, and although the Bible forbids cross-dressing in either sex (Deuteronomy 22:5), the early church fathers taught that a woman gained spirituality by assuming the superior role of a man.[68] St. Jerome wrote, "As long as a woman is for birth and children, she is different from man as body is from soul. But when she wishes to serve Christ more than the world, she will cease to be a woman and will be called man."[69] There have been a number of female transvestite saints; Joan of Arc is the best known.[70] There are no male transvestite saints.

The Popularity of Breeches Parts

In England the fondness for female transvestites continued through the centuries. For example, from the seventeenth century onward, English theater audiences loved to watch pretty young actresses play the part of a man. There was hardly an actress of any note who did not play "breeches parts," as these roles were called.[71] Plays also often included the role of a woman appearing in male disguise. The best known is William Wycherley's *The Plain Dealer,* in which a young woman, who is in love with the hero, Captain Manley, poses as a naval lieutenant and follows Manley to sea.[72] This play, first produced in 1676, is still performed today.

The romantic theme of a beautiful woman dressed as a sailor was so popular that it was even attached to the love story of Emma Hamilton and Horatio Nelson. In the early nineteenth century a most unlikely account circulated that during the time when

Admiral Nelson was with Lord and Lady Hamilton at Palermo, he and Emma Hamilton would dress in the clothes of common sailors and slip out at night to make the rounds of the harbor taverns, "mingling in the sailors' pleasures, listening to their songs, and generally retiring unknown, taking care to settle the score [the check] as they went out."[73]

Society's Tolerance of Lesbianism

In the period we are dealing with—the years between the 1690s and the 1850s—the concept of lesbianism scarcely existed in England. (The word *lesbian* did not come into common usage in England until the twentieth century. An obscure word that dates from the early seventeenth century, *tribade* (from the Greek "to rub"), was used by the literati to identify a woman who had sexual relations with other women, but few people had ever heard the term.)[74]

While it was perfectly acceptable for young women to hug and kiss and hold hands, such shows of affection were not associated with sexual desire. Indeed, what women did among themselves was dismissed as being of little importance. In England there were never laws against sexual acts between women while laws against male homosexual activity were severe.

Lesbianism was not condoned, but it was ignored or denied. Most people went to church and believed what the Bible told them, and the Bible, although far less condemnatory of lesbianism than of male homosexuality, did refer to "the vile passions of women" who "changed the natural use [of their sexuality] into that which is against nature."[75] The clergy, however, seldom mentioned this passage in their sermons, preferring to concentrate on the sins committed by women as prostitutes and seducers of men. The publishers of the biographies of Hannah Snell and Mary Lacy, while hinting at lesbian affairs, were careful to reassure their readers that their heroines were in the final reckoning heterosexual. As we have seen, Hannah Snell's biographer added a fictitious marriage, and in the autobiography of Mary Lacy the publisher not only appended a fictitious marriage but also included a specific, although unconvincing, denial that there was anything sexual in Lacy's relationships with women.[76]

Marriages between Women
In eighteenth-century England, if two women tried to marry and were caught, the license was denied, but they were not prosecuted. Several such cases are found in the registers of marriage brokers in London:

> Married, 1734, December 15: John Mountford of St. Ann's, Soho, Tailor, Bachelor, and Mary Cooper, ditto, Spinster. Suspected 2 women, no certificate.
>
> 20 May 1737: John Smith, Gentleman, of St. James, Westminster, Bachelor, and Elizabeth Huthall, St. Giles, Spinster, at Wilson's. By the opinion after matrimony, my clerk judged they were both women. If the person by name of John Smith be a man, he's a little short fair thin man, not above five foot. After marriage I almost could prove them both women, [although] the one was dressed as a man, thin pale face and wrinkled chin.
>
> 1 October 1747: John Ferren, Gentleman's Servant of St. Andrew's, Holborn, Bachelor, and Deborah Nolan, ditto, Spinster. The supposed John Ferren was discovered after the ceremonies were over to be in person a woman.[77]

The only time a woman who married another woman was prosecuted was when she was accused of other wrongdoing. For example, in 1777 a woman was tried and sentenced "for going in man's clothes and being married to three different women by a fictitious name, and for defrauding them of their money and clothes." It was her having taken their money and possessions that brought on punishment. "She was sentenced to stand in the pillory at Charing Cross and to be imprisoned six months."[78] This was a comparatively light sentence at a time when a person accused of a petty theft could be hanged.

The account of the marriage of the woman seaman known as Samuel Bundy published in the 1760 *Annual Register* illustrates the tolerant attitude of eighteenth-century society toward lesbian relationships. There is no expression of outrage at Bundy's behavior as there would have been if the couple had been male; on the contrary, Bundy is viewed in a most sympathetic light.

Samuel Bundy, aged twenty, married Mary Parlour in a church in Southwark, London, in October 1759. The *Register*'s garbled report first claims that for five months of wedded life Parlour was unaware that Bundy was a woman, accepting Bundy's explanation that illness prevented a consummation of the marriage. Later the article contradicts this statement, saying that "the wife soon discovered the mistake she had made, but was determined for some time not to expose the matter." Bundy revealed the following biographical information to a newspaper reporter:

> Seven years since [at age thirteen] she was seduced from her mother (who then lived, and still lives, near Smithfield [London]), by a limner [an itinerant portrait painter], who debauched her. The day after, to avoid the pursuit of her mother or any discovery of her, should any advertisements [about her abduction] appear, he dressed her in boy's apparel and adopted her for his son by the above name. With him she was a year. At length, they separated, and she took one voyage to sea which kept her employed more than twelve months, in which voyage she performed the several duties of a sailor.[79]

When Bundy returned from sea, still passing as male, "she bound herself to a Mr. Angel, a painter, in the Green Walk near Paris Garden Stairs, in the parish of Christ Church, Surrey," in Southwark. "Whilst with Mr. Angel, she was taken notice of by a young woman [Mary Parlour] who lived at the King's Head in Gravel-lane, Southwark, to whom she was duly married at a neighbouring church." The relationship prospered until Bundy had a dispute with her master and lost her job, whereupon "she was obliged to depend upon her wife for support."[80] When all Mary Parlour's money was spent and Parlour had even pawned her clothes, in a burst of anger she confided to her neighbors that her husband was a woman and had defrauded her of all her earthly goods. To avoid prosecution, Bundy ran away and entered a man-of-war, the *Prince Frederick,* then at Chatham, but soon deserted. Next she joined the crew of a merchant ship, which she found much more to her liking, but she missed Mary Parlour so much, even though Parlour had betrayed her, that she returned to Southwark to see her, knowing that she would be arrested. Bundy was tried, found guilty, and sent to prison for defrauding Parlour of her money and clothes.

Despite Parlour's earlier anger at Bundy, the two were reunited. The *Register* notes, "There [also] seems a strong love and friendship on the other side, as she [Mary Parlour] keeps the prisoner company in her confinement." The article ends with an encomium for Bundy: "The prisoner makes a very good figure as a man; and in her proper dress cannot fail of being a very agreeable woman. She is a very good workwoman at shoemaking and painting; declares she never knew any other man than her seducer; has made herself known, sent for her mother, and appears to be a very sensible woman."[81]

Society's Intolerance of Male Homosexuality

In sharp contrast to the tolerance of intimacy between women, sexual acts between men, from the Middle Ages onward, were punishable by death. (*Sodomy* and *buggery* were the terms used for male homosexuality. The word *homosexuality* came into common usage only in the 1880s.) In the Middle Ages sodomy, together with other sexual sins such as incest, bestiality, and adultery, was tried in an ecclesiastical court, popularly referred to as the bawdy court. Sodomy was punished by torture and death. When, beginning with

Henry VIII, civil courts took over the prosecution of sexual offenses, sodomy continued to be a capital offense, and so it remained until 1861.[82]

Sodomy was one of the few capital crimes in the Royal Navy. The Twenty-ninth Article of War states, "If any person of the fleet shall commit the unnatural and detestable sin of sodomy with man or beast, he shall be punished with death by the sentence of a court martial."[83]

The English had such antipathy to sexual acts between men that even naming such an act was avoided when at all possible, and a great variety of strong adjectives were used to describe the crime or sin: foul, unnatural, detestable, horrid, abominable. This was true over a period of at least seven hundred years. "The Revelations to the Monk of Evesham," written in 1196, referred to homosexuals as "leuyd doers of that foule synne the which oughte not be namyd."[84] Chief Justice Sir Edward Coke (1552–1634) wrote in his definitive work on English law, "Buggery is a detestable and abominable sin, amongst Christians not to be named, committed by carnal knowledge against the ordinance of the Creator, and order of nature, by mankind with mankind, or with brute beast, or by womankind with brute beast." (Notice that carnal knowledge of womankind with womankind is not included.)[85] William Blackstone (1723–80) wrote that "the very mention [of sodomy] is a disgrace to human nature," adding that he would follow "the delicacy of our English law which treats it in its very indictments as a crime not to be named."[86] Similar views were expressed throughout the nineteenth century.

A male homosexual was a threat to the very concept of maleness. He undermined the comforting belief that men, by their very nature, were profound, virile, strong, and direct. A homosexual was stereotyped as effeminate; he, like a woman, was superficial, perverse, weak, and devious.

Englishmen, unlike other European men, did not approve of any show of affection between men. Admiral Sir Thomas Pasley, for example, in his journals covering the period from 1778 to 1782, mentioned his distaste for the way some French officers, prisoners in Pasley's ship, expressed their gratitude for his kindness to them: "I had the honour," he wrote, "of being not only hugged but kissed and slabbered by them. Nasty dogs! I hate a Man's kiss." Again he expressed his dismay when, at a party on board his ship, some Portuguese officers, including a chaplain, "grew warm with liquor before the day was over, and not a little amorous." "I never was," he said, "so hugged and squeezed in my life, absolutely bit in ecstasy by the priest. Beasts!"[87]

The Curious Case of Elizabeth Bowden

In the 1807 court-martial of William Berry, first lieutenant of the sloop *Hazard,* there is an interesting juxtaposition of a young female transvestite serving as chief witness against a man of twenty-two being tried for the capital crime of sodomy. The witness, fourteen-year-old Elizabeth Bowden, had served as a boy, third class, in the crew of the *Hazard.* When "she appeared in court dressed in a long jacket and blue trowsers," neither the naval officers who served on the court nor the press gave any indication that they thought her clothing inappropriate.[88] Not only was her transvestism ignored; no one even suggested that her having served in the navy under a false identity discredited her as a witness.

Elizabeth Bowden was born in Truro, Cornwall. After the death of both her parents, finding herself penniless and alone, she set off on foot from Truro to Plymouth to ask for help from an older sister who had left home some time earlier. When she reached Plymouth she could not find her sister, and according to a newspaper account, "she was obliged through want to disguise herself and volunteer into His Majesty's service."[89]

Early in February 1807 Mistress Bowden, under the name of John Bowden, was entered on the books of the *Hazard,* Captain Charles Dilkes, and she served for six weeks before her gender was discovered.[90] How the discovery was made is not disclosed. When her officers learned that she was a girl, they did not send her ashore. "Since she made known her sex," the *Annual Register* noted, "the captain and officers have paid every attention to her; they gave her an apartment to sleep in, and she still remains on board the *Hazard* as an attendant on the officers of the ship."[91] She was still on board at the time of the court-martial and was identified in the proceedings as a member of the crew.

The court-martial of Lieutenant Berry took place in the *Salvador del Mundo* on 2 and 3 October 1807 in the waters of the Hamoaze, off Plymouth. Berry was charged with having committed, on 23 August 1807 on board the sloop *Hazard,* "the unnatural and detestable sin of sodomy with Thomas Gibbs, a boy of the second class belonging to the said sloop, punishable by the Twenty-ninth Article of War." He was further accused "of having frequently been guilty with the said Thomas Gibbs of that part of the Second Article of War relating to [moral] uncleanness or other scandalous actions."[92]

The crime occurred on a lazy summer Sunday as the vessel was returning to Plymouth, with the men relaxing after their week's work. Bowden was idling away her off-duty hours when the boy Gibbs, a servant to the gunroom mess, was called into Lieutenant Berry's cabin. The cabin door was then shut. (Gibbs's age is not given, but he was under fourteen; otherwise he would have been tried for sodomy together with Berry.)[93] Bowden decided to see what was going on. She sneaked down to Berry's cabin door.

The court record gives her testimony:

Elizabeth, alias John Bowden (a girl), borne on the *Hazard*'s books as a boy of the third class, was sworn and examined:

Prosecutor: Did you ever, during the time you have been on board the *Hazard,* look through the keyhole of Mr. Berry's cabin door and see the boy Thomas Gibbs in any way in an indecent manner employed with his hands with the prisoner?

Berry: Yes, a little before we came in [to Plymouth harbor]. I looked through the keyhole and I saw Thomas Gibbs playing with the prisoner's privates. I went up and called the gunroom steward and told him to come down and look through the keyhole and see what they were about. He did come down, but did not look in and called me aloft and told me to sit down.

Prosecutor: Have you frequently observed Thomas Gibbs go into the prisoner's cabin, and the door shut, and the prisoner at the same time in the cabin?

Berry: Yes.

Prosecutor: Did Thomas Gibbs ever relate to you or in your hearing what passed between him and the prisoner? And what induced you to look through the keyhole?

Berry: Gibbs has never told me anything that has happened—he was called in several times, and I thought I would see what he was about.

Prosecutor: Are you sure that it was the prisoner's private parts that you saw Thomas Gibbs have hold of?

Berry: Yes.

Court [one of the officers judging the case]: What light was there in the cabin at the time?

Berry: One candle.

The witness withdrew.[94]

The case against Lieutenant Berry was far from clear. John Hoskin, the gunroom steward, whom Bowden had summoned to Berry's door, testified that the boy Gibbs was a thief and a liar; he had stolen from Berry and other officers and then refused to admit it. Berry denied all the charges. He said that Gibbs had brought the false accusations as revenge after Berry threatened to thrash him.

The court adjudged the charges fully proved, and on 19 October 1807 Berry was hanged at the starboard fore-yardarm of the *Hazard*.[95] Nothing further is known about Elizabeth Bowden.

Society's Attitudes Summarized

Although there were exceptions, society's attitude toward the transvestism of women seaman was one of tolerant amusement. A woman's cross-dressing was viewed as a harmless masquerade rather
than as a serious attempt to storm the bastions of male dominance.
While male homosexuality was a capital offense, there were no laws
against sexual relations between women. The public liked the image
of the delicate young woman who acquired a male role and went
to sea to find her lost lover. More likely motives—that a woman
joined the navy or marines in order to improve her social and economic status, to escape the tedium or unpleasantness of her situation on land, or because she identified with men—were ignored.

THE LAST OF THE WOMEN SEAMEN

The latest case I have found of a woman in male disguise joining
the navy is that of William Brown, the black woman mentioned at
the beginning of this chapter, who served from around 1804 to
around 1816. After 1815, following the close of the wars with
France and the United States, the British Royal Navy was greatly
reduced in size. Without the need to raise huge numbers of men,
officers could be discriminating in choosing their crews; they
checked the background of newly entered men, so that it became
much more difficult for a recruit to hide his, or her, identity. As the
nineteenth century progressed, there were routine physical examinations upon entry, and regulations required the men to bathe and
change their underclothes regularly. It became impossible for a
woman to hide her gender.

This does not mean that women would not have continued to
join the navy and marines if they could. There are several recorded cases of women passing as men in merchant ships and whalers
in the mid-nineteenth century, but they do not concern us here.[96]

CHAPTER 4

The Story of Mary Lacy, Alias William Chandler

Oh when I was a fair maid about seventeen
I enlisted in the Navy for to serve the Queen.
I enlisted in the Navy, a sailor for to stand,
For to hear the cannons rattling, and the music so grand.
. . . .
They sent me to bed, and they sent me to bunk,
To lie with the sailors, I never was afraid.
But putting off my blue coat, it often made me smile
To think I'd laid with a thousand men, and a maiden all the while.

—"When I Was a Fair Maid"

ON A SPRING DAY IN 1759 the servant girl Mary Lacy decided to run away from home. She explains in her autobiography, "A thought came into my head to dress myself in men's apparel and set off by myself, but where to go I did not know, nor what I was to do when I was gone." What she did was join the Royal Navy for what proved to be a twelve-year stint.

Lacy published her autobiography, *The History of the Female Shipwright,* in 1773 in conjunction with a London publisher and printer, M. Lewis.[1] Three abbreviated editions were issued in the United States in the early nineteenth century.[2] Then her story was forgotten.

Muster books confirm that she did indeed serve in the ships she tells about, and Admiralty minutes note that she served seven years as an apprentice at Portsmouth Dockyard and then worked there as a fully qualified shipwright. In contrast to Hannah Snell and Mary Anne Talbot, Mary Lacy never became a celebrity; there is no clue to what became of her after her book was published.

No portrait exists, and she never described her own appearance. We only know that she was of small stature and that she easily passed for a boy. When she was in her late twenties and working at Portsmouth Dockyard under the name William Chandler, her fellow workers described her as a "little man" whose girlfriend was too large for "him." When it was rumored that Chandler was a girl, the men of the yard found it hard to believe: "There is not," they said, "the least appearance of it in the make or shape of him." Unlike most of her fellow seamen, Lacy was literate and could write down her story herself; she has a galloping, no-nonsense style that is easy to identify. Occasionally, however, a passage is interjected that has a different tone, stilted and sermonizing, and it is probable that these sections were inserted by the publisher Lewis or a hireling of his in a clumsy attempt to discount Lacy's lesbian propensities. An example is found in the book's preface:

> It will not be amiss to conclude this address by explaining my motives for endeavoring to be as frequently as possible in the company of women in the way of courtship, which were: In the first place, to avoid the conversation of the men, which I need not observe, was amongst those of this class [seafaring men] especially, in many respects, very offensive to a delicate ear; and, secondly, for the sake of affording me a more agreeable repast amongst persons of my own sex, many of whom, I am sorry to say, were too much addicted to evil practices by their unlawful

commerce with the other [sex], as will on many occasions appear in the course of the story.

It seems that Lewis, while well aware that Lacy's anecdotes of her amorous adventures with women would increase book sales, felt it necessary to make a token bow to morality, especially since a lot of his profits came from publications of puritanical religious groups such as the well-funded Moravian Brethren.[3] He wavered. In the text above, after his peculiar apologia for Lacy's courting of women, he could not resist adding a titillating forecast of her adventures with prostitutes and other errant females.

Mary Lacy felt no such ambivalence. She took on the guise of a man with the greatest enthusiasm, never questioning her right or ability to do so. In fact, she was so comfortable in her male role that as one reads her text, it is easy to forget that she was a woman. Except for the note in the preface, she did not dissemble about her flirtations with women. Women of all ages were attracted to her, and she to them.

It may have been Lewis who placed special emphasis on Lacy's teenage crush on a young man she met at a dance while she was still working as a domestic servant. In several passages it is explained that she ran away from home in order to find respite from her lovelorn state. From the text as a whole, however, it is evident that she left home because she resented the restrictions of her life as a nursemaid, and because she liked the idea of acquiring a male identity, which she could not do in her home town.

Lewis may also be responsible for the addition of what could be a bit of fiction added at the very end of the autobiography: a claim that after Lacy resigned from the navy she married a "Mr. Slade" (no first name is given). More about that later.

Because Mary Lacy's autobiography is the only reliable firsthand account of naval life written by an eighteenth-century woman seaman, it seems worthwhile to give extensive excerpts from her book,

but to reproduce here all 191 pages of her story would be excessive.
I have tried to select the most representative anecdotes from each
period of her career, and to skip material that is not pertinent to
our subject. Lacy herself so clearly reveals her goals, her attitudes,
and her opinions that her text needs little editorial comment.

The book begins:

> After mentioning my maiden name, which was Mary Lacy, it will
> be proper to inform the reader that I was born at Wickham, in
> the county of Kent, on the twelfth of January, 1740; but had not
> been long in the world before my father and mother agreed to
> live at Ash, so that I knew little more of Wickham than I had
> learned from my parents, on which account Ash might almost
> be reckoned my native place.
>
> My father and mother were poor, and forced to work very
> hard for their bread. They had one son and two daughters, of
> whom I was the eldest. At the proper time, my mother put me
> to school, to give me what learning she could, which kept me out
> of their way whilst they were at work; for being young, I was
> always in mischief; and my mother not having spare time suffi-
> cient to look after me, I had so much of my own will that when
> I came to have some knowledge, it was a difficult matter for
> them to keep me within proper bounds.
>
> After I had learned my letters, I was admitted into a charity
> school, which was kept by one Mrs. R——n; and she, knowing
> my parents, took great pains to instruct me in reading. As I took
> my learning very fast, my mistress was the more careful of me;
> for she was indeed as a mother to me; and in these respects was
> more serviceable than my parents could possibly be.
>
> When I was old enough to learn to work, my mistress taught
> me to knit; which she perceiving me very fond of learning,
> employed me in knitting gloves, stockings, nightcaps, and such
> sort of work so that I soon perfected myself in it; which I was the
> more encouraged to as my mistress rewarded me for every piece
> of knitting, and all the money I earned she reserved in a little
> box; so that when I wanted anything, she would buy it for me.

Thus, by the help of God and good friends, I was no great charge to my parents; for being always at school, my mistress set me about all manner of work in the house; so that, though young, I was very handy, and in a way of improvement.[4]

About this time I used to go on errands for my neighbors, and help them [with] what I could; but that practice, by occasioning me to go pretty much abroad in the streets, became very prejudicial to me for I was thereby addicted to all manner of mischief, as will appear by the following instance: There was one C——h——e Cipp——r about my age that lived in Ash with whom, when I could get out, I always kept company, and when together [we] did many unjustifiable actions. One day we took it into our heads to purloin a bridle and saddle out of the stable of Mr. John R——n, butcher at Ash, who kept a little horse in a field about half a mile from the town. This horse we caught, put the saddle and bridle on, and rode about the field till we were tired, and afterwards restored them to the place from whence we took them.

I liked riding so well that I never was easy but when among the horses; for I used to go to Mr. R——h——d——n and say, "Master, shall I fetch your sheep up out of the field?" And if he wanted them, I immediately took the little horse, without saddle or bridle, and mounting on his back, set off as fast as the horse could go, thus running all hazards of my life; and was so wild and heedless that if anybody took notice of my riding so fast, and told me I should fall off and break my neck, my answer was, "Neck or nothing!"

During Lacy's childhood her mother was the most important person in her life. She scarcely mentions her father or her siblings:

I then thought my mother was my greatest enemy; for being a very passionate woman, [she] used to beat me in such a manner that the neighbors thought she would kill me. But after my crying was over, I was out of the doors again at my old tricks with my playfellows and frequently stayed out all day long and never went home at all, for which I was afterwards to be corrected.

At about the age of twelve Lacy entered domestic service, and for the next seven years she lived and worked in a series of households in Ash. Although her employers treated her well, she fretted under the restrictions imposed on her liberty by her long hours of household duties: "I was so very thoughtless and discontented," she explained, "that I was always ill or had some complaint or other to make…. Being of a roving disposition, I never liked to be within doors."

In her later teenage years Lacy often sneaked out of her employers' residence to "be dancing all the night long" at a house where a musician played the violin "for the young men and maids of the town" to dance to, and she became enamored of one of her dancing partners:

> I now embraced all opportunities of going out to dance with my sweetheart, for when I was with him I imagined myself happy. But this young man did not perceive that I loved him so much, and it happened very unfortunately I did not tell any of my friends of it, which if I had done, it would probably have been better for me, for my mother would no doubt have persuaded me [to forget the young man] for my good. But I afterwards felt the bad effects of concealing this warm affection. I could not blame the young man since he had never given me any reason for to do.
>
> Hereupon I was very unsettled in my mind, and unable to fix myself in any place; nevertheless, I carried it off as well as I could….
>
> But my mind became continually disturbed and uneasy about this young man, who was the involuntary cause of all my trouble, which was aggravated by my happening to see him one day talk to a young woman: the thoughts of this made me so very unhappy that I was from that time more unsettled than ever.

Later in the text Lacy harks back to her infatuation with this young man with a warning against flirtations with the opposite sex:

I shall here take an opportunity of advising all maidens never to give their minds to frequent the company of young men, or to seem fond of them, and I would also caution them not to addict themselves to dancing with the male sex as I wantonly did. But had I been in bed and asleep, which I ought to have been, the unknown sorrows I have since felt and experienced would not have befallen me. But then I was young and foolish and had not the thought or care of an older person. I would likewise admonish all young men to beware how they marry; for I have seen so much of my own sex that it is enough for a man to hate them. However, there are good and bad of both sexes.

A short time after, a thought came into my head to dress myself in men's apparel and set off by myself; but where to go I did not know, nor what I was to do when I was gone. I had no thought what was to become of me, or what sorrow and anxiety I should bring upon my aged father and mother because of me; but my inclinations were still bent on leaving home.

In order to do this I went one day into my master's brother's room, and there found an old frock [coat], an old pair of breeches, an old pair of pumps, and an old pair of stockings, all of which did very well. But still [I] was at a great loss for a hat. But then I recollected that my father had got one at home if I could but procure it unknown to my parents; I therefore intended to get it without their knowledge. Whereupon I went to my mother's house to ask her for a gown which I had given her the day before to mend for me. She answered, I should have it tomorrow. But little did my poor mother know what I wanted; for I went immediately into my father's room, took the hat, put it under my apron, and came downstairs. But I never said goodbye or anything else to my mother, but went home to my place [the house where she worked] and packed up the things that I had got, and now only waited an opportunity to decamp.

On the first day of May, 1759, about six o'clock in the morning, I set off, and when I had got out of town into the fields, I pulled off my clothes and put on the men's, leaving my own in a hedge, some in one place and some in another.

Having thus dressed myself in men's habit, I went on to a place called Wingham where a fair was held that day. Here I wandered about till evening; then went to a public house and asked them to let me have a lodging that night for which I agreed to give two pence. Now all the money I had when I came away was five pence.

Accordingly, I went to bed and slept very well till morning, when I got up and began to think which way I should go, as my money was so short; however, I proceeded toward Canterbury.

She hitched a ride on the back of a post chaise (a horse-drawn carriage), "not knowing whither I was going, never having been so far from home in my life," and rode first to Canterbury, then onward to what turned out to be Chatham, where one of the great naval dockyards was located:

> When the chaise had reached Chatham, I got down but was an utter stranger to the place, only I remembered to have heard my father and mother talking about a man's being hung in chains at Chatham; and when I saw him, I thought this must be the place.

This was merely coincidence. Lacy was not aware that in all the larger towns of England, corpses of felons were hung in chains as a reminder to the populace of the fate of lawbreakers.

At Chatham she spent her last penny on bread and cheese and so had no money to pay for lodging:

> I walked up and down the streets, as it was the fair time, and sauntered about till it was dark. As I stood considering what I should do, I looked about me and saw a farmhouse on the left hand of Chatham as you go down the hill. I thought within myself I would go to it and ask them to let me lie there, but when I came down to the house, I was ashamed to make the request.

In this distressed situation I continued some time, not knowing how to proceed; for money I had none, and to lie in the
streets I never was used to, and what to do I did not know.
But at last I resolved to lie in the straw [in the barnyard close
to the farmer's pigs], concluding that to be somewhat better than
lying in the street.... [Throughout the night] I was afraid to
move, for when the pigs stirred a little, I thought someone was
coming to frighten me. Therefore, I did not dare to open my eyes
lest I should see something frightful. I had but very little sleep.

When it was morning, I got up and shook my clothes and
looked about to see if anybody perceived me get out. I then came
down to the town and went up to some men that belonged to a
collier [a coal-carrying vessel] who gave me some victuals and
drink with them.

While I was standing here, a gentleman came up to me and
asked me if I would go to sea, "for," said he, "it is fine weather
now at sea, and if you will go, I will get you a good master on
board the *Sandwich*."

I replied, "Yes, sir."

The *Sandwich*, a ninety-gun ship of the line, had recently been
launched at Chatham and had not yet collected a crew, although a
few of the warrant officers were already living on board.[5] At this
time the navy was desperate for men. England was in the third year
of the Seven Years' War against the French. Naval ships were fighting in North America, the West Indies, Africa, and India, and at
home, only the navy stood between Great Britain and a French
invasion.[6] It was a happy surprise for a naval recruiter to come
upon a healthy young volunteer.

He then showed me the nearest way on board, but instead of
going to St. Princess's bridge (as the gentleman had directed me),
I went over where the tide came up, being half up my legs in
mud. But at length I got up to the bridge and seeing the boat
there I asked the men belonging to it if they were going on board
the *Sandwich*. They told me they were and asked me if I wanted

to go on board. I told them yes. They inquired who I wanted there. I told them the gunner. They laughed, said I was a brave boy and that I would do very well for him. But I did not know who was to be my master, or what I was to do, or whether I had strength to perform it. They then carried me on board.... When getting out of the lighter into the *Sandwich*, I thought it was impossible for such a great ship to go to sea.

Lacy was directed to the gunner:

When the gunner saw me he asked where I came from and how I came there. I told him I had left my friends. He inquired if I had been 'prentice to anybody and run away. I told him no.

"Well," said he, "Should you like to go to sea?"

I replied, "Yes, sir."

He then asked if I was hungry. I answered in the affirmative, having had but little all the day. Upon this he ordered his servant to serve me some biscuit and cheese. The boy went and brought me some and said, "Here, countryman, eat heartily," which I accordingly did; for the biscuit being new, I liked it well, or else my being hungry made it go down very sweet and savory.

The gunner's servant was Jeremiah Paine, a young man about Lacy's age who soon became her good friend.[7]

After I had eat sufficiently, the gunner came and asked my name. I told him my name was WILLIAM CHANDLER, but God knows how that name came into my head, though it is true that my mother's maiden name was Chandler, and my father's name is William Lacy....

I had been on board the *Sandwich* about four days when the carpenter came on board. He had only one servant who was at work in Chatham Yard, so that at that time he had none on board. The gunner told me the carpenter would be glad to have me as his servant. He [the gunner] was not willing I should be the captain's servant, that being the worst place in the ship; but at that time I did not know which was the best or the worst.

The gunner, together with his fellow warrant officers, was envious of the number of servants allowed the ship's captain and the special privileges they received. He was not about to pass a lively young lad over to a commissioned officer.

> Mr. [William] Russel, the gunner, spoke to Mr. Richard Baker, the carpenter, for me.[8]

Baker accepted Mary, alias William, as his servant and began at once to teach her her duties:

> He first of all ordered me to fetch him a can [a mug] of beer. I accordingly went and brought it to him.
>
> "Now," said he, "you must learn to make me a can of flip [a heated mixture of beer, spirits, and sugar], and to broil me a beefsteak, and to make my bed. Come, I will show you how to make my bed."
>
> So we went to his cabin, in which there was a bed that turned up [a hammock], and he began to take the bedclothes off one by one.
>
> "Now," said he, "you must shake them one by one, you must tumble and shake the bed about, then you must lay the sheets on, one at a time, and lastly, the blankets."
>
> I replied, "Yes, sir."
>
> "Well," said he, "you will soon learn to make a bed, that I see already."
>
> But he little knew who he had got to make his bed. He not having any suspicion of my being a woman, I affected to appear as ignorant of the matter as if I had known nothing about it.
>
> He then provided for me a bed and bedding and directed his mate to sling it up for me.
>
> When I attempted to get into bed at night, I got in at one side and fell out at the other, which made all the seamen laugh at me. But, as it happened, there were not a great many on board, for being a new ship, but few had entered on board of her. My hammock was hung up in the sun deck, but [later] when the whole ship's company was on board, it was taken down and placed

below in the wing where the carpenter and the yeomen both were. Now it was better for me to lay there than anywhere else, but I was very uneasy lying there on account of a quartermaster that lay in that place whom I did not much like.

Lacy's use of the word *uneasy* suggests that the man was sexually threatening; attacks on ship's boys were not uncommon.

And when I came to lie in the blankets, I did not know what to do, for I thought I was eat up with vermin, having been on board ten days and had no clothes to shift myself with, so that I looked black enough to frighten anybody.

Baker was proud of his status as ship's carpenter and wanted to make sure that his servant reflected well on him. Lacy noted later in the book:

He always caused me clean my own shoes as well as those that belonged to him, and if they were not done to his mind, he would kick me with great violence. Whereupon he peremptorily expressed himself thus: "You dog, I will make you go neat and clean, for you are a carpenter's servant and you shall appear as such."

Baker directed Mary to visit him at his house in Chatham to get a bath and some decent clothes. When she arrived there, he was sitting in the kitchen, and he asked her if she was hungry.

Indeed I thought I could gladly eat a bit of bread and butter and drink a basin of tea, for I even longed for some [tea], having had none since I came away from Ash. But I told him I was not hungry; notwithstanding which, he, being a merry man, said to me, "You can eat a little bit."

I answered, "Yes, sir."

On my saying this, my mistress gave me a basin of tea and a bit of bread and butter, more than I could eat, but I quickly found a way to dispose of the remainder, for what I could not eat I put in my pocket.

When I had eat my breakfast, my master called me out back-wards, where there was some soap and water to wash myself with. How glad was I, hardly being able to contain myself for joy. But there was something that gave me greater pleasure, for after I had washed myself, my mistress gave me a clean shirt, a pair of stockings, a pair of shoes, a coat and waistcoat, a checked handkerchief, and a red nightcap for me to wear at sea. I was also to have my hair cut off when I went on board, but this operation I did not like at all, yet was afraid to say anything to my master about it.

Her mistress also bought her two checked shirts and a pair of shoes:

Therefore, I thought that I was a sailor, every inch of me.

Baker had a chest made for Mary to store her clothes in, warning her that she should keep it locked, for the seamen would steal the teeth out of her head if they could.

After this my master began to teach me the nature of the ship and how to cook for him, which gave me an opportunity of dis-covering his natural temper. Sometimes on mere trifling occa-sions he was very hot when things were not according to his mind. On that account I was always afraid of him, and when he was in a passion [I] stood with the cabin door in my hand in order to make an escape, which, when I did, he always beat me. This usage I could hardly brook when I knew that I was as real a woman as his mother. Besides, when at home, I could not bear to be spoke to, much less to have my faults told me. But now I found it was come to blows and thought it was very hard to be struck by a man; which occasioned me to reflect that there was a wide difference between being at home and in my present sit-uation abroad.

On 20 May 1759 the *Sandwich* sailed to Black Stakes to take in her guns, and on 10 June she moved to the Nore, where the remainder of her crew were collected.[9] She had a complement of 750 men.

We had now got a great number of men on board; some we had from the *Polly Green,* some from one ship, and some from another. These men were paid off from the several ships to come on board of us.[10]

While we lay at the Nore, there came a bumboat woman on board of us to sell all sorts of goods. This woman, being an acquaintance of my master, had the use of his cabin, and I was desired to boil the teakettle for her and to do anything she ordered me. I was glad of it, for she was very good to me and gave me a new purse to put my money in. Now my master kept the key of the roundhouse [where the women living in the crew's quarters went to the toilet]...and he told me not to let them have the key unless they gave me something. By this means I got several pence from them.

On 21 June the *Sandwich* set out to join Admiral Edward Hawke's large squadron blockading the harbor of Brest where the French fleet was gathered, and in July Rear Admiral Francis Geary and his large retinue transferred to the *Sandwich.*[11]

In the navy of this era it was the practice to include among the numerous servants of admirals and captains a special group of "young gentlemen" drawn from the upper classes who were not servants in the usual sense but were training to become commissioned officers. These snooty boys considered it a prerogative of their superior social station to bully the lower-class boys who served the boatswain, the gunner, and the carpenter. The young gentlemen serving Admiral Geary were no exception:

Among the admiral's servants there were a great number of stout boys, very wicked and mischievous,...[who] were every now and then trying to pick a quarrel with me....

One day being sent down to the galley to broil a beefsteak, one of these audacious boys, whose name was William Severy, came and gave me a slap in the face that made me reel.... Lieutenant Cook [the ship's cook], knowing me better than any of them,...told me I should fight him and, if conqueror, should have a plum pudding, and that he would, in the meantime, mind the steak. Upon which I went aft to the main hatchway and pulled off my jacket, but they wanted me to pull off my shirt, which I would not suffer for fear of it being discovered that I was a woman, and it was with much difficulty that I could keep it on.

Hereupon we instantly engaged and fought a great while, but during the combat, he threw me such violent cross-buttocks... [as] were almost enough to dash my brains out, but I never gave out, for I knew that if I did I should have one or other of them continually upon me. Therefore, we kept to it with great obstinacy on both sides, and I soon began to get the advantage of my antagonist, which all the people who knew me perceiving, seemed greatly pleased, especially when he declined fighting any more, and the more so because he was looked upon as the best fighter among them. This contest ending favorably for me, I reigned master over the rest, they being all afraid of me; and it was a most lucky circumstance that I had spirit and vigor to conquer him who was my greatest adversary, for if I had not I should have been [so] harassed and ill treated amongst them that my very life would have been a burden.

As soon as I had put myself in some tolerable order, I went for the steak and carried it to [my master's] cabin, being a little afraid that I should be chastised.

"Well," said he, "you have been a long while about the steak, I hope it is well done now."

"Yes, sir," said I.

"Why," says he, looking very attentively, "I suppose you have been fighting?"

I answered, "Yes, sir, I was forced to fight or else be drubbed."

"But," said he, "I hope you have not been beat."

I replied, "No, sir."

Upon the whole I came off with flying colors. From this time, the boy and I who fought became as well reconciled to one another as if we had been brothers, and he always let me share what he had.

One day Lacy saw some of the seamen dictating letters home and decided she would write to her parents, whom she had not contacted since running away two months before:

I could write but very indifferently, but to entrust any person with my thoughts on this occasion I imagined would be very improper.

She composed the following letter, dated 3 July 1759:

Honorable Father and Mother,

This comes with my duty to you, and hope that you are both in good health, as I am at present, thanks be to God for it. I would have you make yourselves as easy as you can, for I have got a very good master who is carpenter on board the *Sandwich,* and am now upon the French Coast, right over Brest. Shall be glad to hear from you as soon as you can. So no more at present from,

Your undutiful daughter,

Mary Lacy

P.S. Please to direct [letters] thus: *For William Chandler on board the* Sandwich *at Brest.*

Six weeks later she received an answer from her mother, who was so relieved to know that Mary was alive that she made no mention of the startling fact that her daughter not only had adopted a male identity but had joined the navy. Her letter begins:

My dear child,

I received yours safe and was glad to hear that you are in good health, but I have been at death's door mostly with grief for you. Your clothes, after your departure, were found in a hedge, which occasioned me to think you were murdered. I have had no rest day or night, for I thought that if you had been alive, you would have written to me before.

In the meantime, Lacy was stricken with a severe attack of what she called rheumatism; it was probably a form of rheumatoid arthritis. (She was to suffer from this disease on and off for the rest of her naval career and ultimately was forced to resign because of it.) When she showed Baker her swollen fingers, he thought that she had gout, from which he himself suffered. It was then believed that gout was caused by too much rich food and port wine:

> He fell a-laughing at me, adding, "Hang me if William is not growing rich. You dog, you have got the gout in your fingers."

It was no joke to Lacy. Her legs swelled to the point where she could not walk. She was carried down to the sick bay, "a nasty, unwholesome place." Her master sent her tea and buttered biscuits as a special treat every day, but this was little comfort, for she received her food from the hands of an old man "who was of so uncleanly a disposition that had I been ever so well, I could not have relished it from him." She grew worse and worse "and was much altered."

After several weeks she sent word to her master that she would die if she remained in the sick bay. He arranged to have her brought up to his cabin for several hours each day, and she began to recover, but she was very lame for a long time:

> My master got me crutches with a spike at each end for my safety to walk about on the deck, and when anybody affronted me in an ill-natured way, I used to throw my crutch at them.

Baker used to tease her, saying that in a battle she would not be able to bring up the gunpowder fast enough.

> I replied, "I'll take it from the little boys, and cause them to fetch more before the gun shall want powder," at which he laughed heartily to hear me talk so, as he well might.

To spend months at sea patrolling the Bay of Biscay was both tedious and perilous. The bay was notorious for its contrary winds and dangerous coasts, and English charts were not always accurate. The rallying point of the squadron was just off the island of Ushant at the entrance to the English Channel, an especially dangerous position. Sailing ships were cautioned not even to come within sight of the island's treacherous rocks; a French proverb warned, "Who sees Ushant sees his own blood."[12] And perhaps because the *Sandwich* was a new ship, constructed in the rush of wartime with improperly seasoned wood, she was less seaworthy than other vessels, and her crew were especially afflicted with illness.

On 29 August 1759 the *Sandwich* had to go to Plymouth for repairs and to send her sick to the hospital. She returned to her station at the end of September.[13] As the autumn stormy season progressed, one gale was quickly followed by another. Crews were not only exhausted from fighting to keep their ships from being wrecked; they were also suffering from lack of fresh food and beer, for it was proving difficult for the victualing ships sent out from England to get supplies on board the blockading vessels in the rough seas.

Lacy made no specific comments on these storm-ridden months. She only remarked in passing:

> A person who is a stranger to these great and boisterous seas would think it impossible for a large ship to ride in them; but I slept many months on the ocean where I have been tossed up and down at an amazing rate.

On 7 October the *Sandwich*, battling a storm, sprang her maintopmast; other ships were also damaged. On the twelfth, in the continuing westerly gale, the fleet sailed for Plymouth for repairs and victualing, leaving only a few of the frigates to watch the French fleet. Hawke assured the Admiralty that "while this wind shall continue it is impossible for the enemy to stir."[14] This time he was right.

On 7 November another furious westerly gale drove the fleet from their station. They sought shelter at Torbay.[15] On the way there, however, the *Sandwich* once again sprang her mainmast and shredded her sails so that she could not be maneuvered into the harbor. She spent the night of the eleventh fighting the storm off the dangerous Devon coast. Lieutenant Baker's report in his log was wistful: "The fleet anchored in Torbay, but we was obliged to keep the sea."[16] When, on 14 November, most of Hawke's ships cleared Torbay to return to Ushant, the *Sandwich* and two other storm-disabled vessels had to go to Plymouth for repairs, and the *Sandwich*, as before, needed to get her sick seamen to the hospital.

On the fifteenth Hawke learned that, contrary to his expectations, the French fleet had come out of Brest Harbor, and he guessed correctly that they were headed south for Quiberon Bay to pick up the soldiers who were gathered there awaiting the planned invasion of Great Britain. Hawke's ships set out in hot pursuit.

The same day, Geary wrote to the secretary of the Admiralty from Plymouth:

> Please acquaint their Lordships that I arrived here this morning in His Majesty's Ship *Sandwich*, in company with the *Ramillies* and *Anson*, in pursuance of an order from Sir Edward Hawke...and so soon as I can possibly get the sick out of the ship and receive others in lieu, and have got a new maintopmast, maintopsail yard and sails in lieu of what was sprung and split in the last gale of wind, together with the stores and provisions completed, I shall proceed with the utmost dispatch to rejoin Sir Edward Hawke, whom I parted company with last night at 10 o'clock off the Start [Start Point south of Torbay] with a fine breeze of wind at N.N.E.[17]

The following day he informed the Admiralty that he would sail "this night or tomorrow morning."[18] No such luck! A new gale came on, and the ships could not get under way. On 17 November Geary learned that the French fleet was at sea, but it was not until the nineteenth that he at last got out of Plymouth Sound. The *Sandwich* did not reach Quiberon Bay until 22 November, two days after Hawke had caught up with and destroyed the French fleet. Thus Mary Lacy missed participating in the Battle of Quiberon Bay, one of the great naval victories in the history of England.

Hawke's decisive defeat of the French navy ended the threat of an invasion of England, but the war was still on, and the blockade of the French coast continued. In December the *Sandwich* was patrolling off Brest when she received Hawke's orders to join him at Quiberon. Geary dutifully set off amid heavy squalls. First the *Sandwich* was driven by easterly gales far into the Atlantic. On 15 December she was 480 miles west-northwest of Ushant. Then, as she worked her way back, she was hit by a new gale, this time from the southwest, and was very nearly wrecked on the French coast east of Ushant.[19] Finally, on the day after Christmas she staggered into Spithead from where Geary wrote to the Admiralty to explain what in heaven she was doing there:

> As the upper works, sides and decks of the *Sandwich* are very leaky and the oakum worked out of all the waterways of the seams upon every deck, in so much that the officers and ship's company lay wet, whenever it rains...and having upward of 120 sick on board, 100 of whom are in fevers, the scurvy, fluxes, and consumptions, that the surgeon says there is an absolute necessity of their being sent to the hospital; the beer having been out some days, and having no wine or brandy on board, and in want of sails and stores; I judged it absolutely necessary, as the wind was southerly and I could not recover my station, to bear up for the first port.[20]

By January 1760 the *Sandwich* was back on patrol. While Lacy wrote very little about these desperate months, she did describe a shore visit:

> As we were stationed off Cape Finisterre and the wind blowing so hard that we could not lie there, we afterwards went and anchored in Quiberon Bay, and when there the officers went frequently on shore; which our master perceiving, obtained leave for me to go with the admiral's boys when an opportunity offered.... We had a great deal of pleasure in walking about the island in the daytime; but there were very few people in it. When they saw our boat coming on shore, they sent the young women out of the island for fear of our officers; and there were left remaining only two or three old men, and one old woman.

On 12 February the *Sandwich, Ramillies, Royal William,* and five other ships were sailing together down the channel when "a dreadful hurricane arose which lasted two days." (Lacy is a month off on the date; she gives it as 12 January.)

> By reason of this storm we lost sight of each other, not knowing where we were, and the sea running mountains high, all of us expected to perish. We had seven men drowned, had sprung our main and foremast, and were very nigh the land, but as it pleased God to give us a sight of the danger we were in, we very happily kept clean of the land, and next day went into Plymouth Sound.
>
> When my master went on shore into the yard to report the damage of the ship, I went with him, and we were greatly affected on seeing that only twenty-five men were saved out of seven hundred that were in the *Ramillies,* which was lost on the fourteenth of January. [She was in fact wrecked on Bolt Head 15 February.][21]
>
> The *Sandwich* was ordered to the shipyard for repairs, which I was glad of, as I always went on shore with my master, who frequented the Sign of the Cross Keys at North Conner.

Lacy was happy to have a respite from the hard months at sea, but she was finding Baker increasingly difficult. His pay was no doubt in arrears, and he was drinking heavily:

> When my master was sober, he would sit down and reckon what money he had spent, the thoughts of which ruffled his temper greatly, and at such times I was always the chief object of his resentment; therefore, I was sorry when he was not in liquor.
>
> I now thought that if I could get clear of the ship, I would esteem myself happy, but recollected I had no money; for my master had never paid me any [servants' wages went to their masters]; and my clothes were made out of old canvas. When I was served with wine, I sold it at two shillings a bottle, and that helped provide me some shirts.

Clothes were important to Lacy; not only her social status but her very existence as a man depended on her attire. She was therefore especially distressed that Baker no longer made the effort to see that she was properly dressed. He did, however, "make many fair promises":

> Amongst others [he promised] that he would bind me out [a carpenter's] 'prentice and clothe me during that time, though I could never believe it would come to anything.

In the autumn of 1760, while the *Sandwich* was at Portsmouth, Lacy suffered a renewed attack of her rheumatic complaint and was taken to the hospital. Although she was there for some time, the only treatment she received was to be bled, and no one discovered that she was a woman.[22]

By the time she was released, the *Sandwich* had sailed, so she was assigned as a supernumerary in the one-hundred-gun guardship *Royal Sovereign*, stationed at Spithead.[23] This proved a blessing for Lacy. She was now free of the irascible Baker, and soon after she went on board Admiral Geary, newly appointed port admiral of Portsmouth, moved to the *Royal Sovereign*, together with his servants, who had been friends with Lacy in the *Sandwich*, and, she remarks, "they were glad to see me."[24]

She made new friends as well. A young woman living on board with one of Lacy's messmates, John Grant, became her close companion:

> The young woman and I were very intimate, and as she was exceeding fond of me, we used to play together like young children.... Our messmates believed we were too familiar together, but neither of us regarded their surmises, and if they said anything to her, she told them that if anything like what they suspected had passed between us, the same should be practiced in future.
>
> However, when John Grant became acquainted that she and I were so fond of each other's company, he began to be somewhat displeased. Nevertheless, he was afraid to take any notice of it lest his messmates should laugh at him. Yet though he

seemed to wink at it, he showed her several tokens of his resentment by beating her and otherwise using her very ill, threatening to send her on shore.

One day when Lacy was working on deck she tripped over a cable and fell through an open grate into the hold; her head hit a cask and was badly cut. She was carried to the surgeon's quarters, and he sewed up the wound:

> When I came to myself I was very apprehensive lest the doctor in searching for bruises about my body should have discovered that I was a woman, but it fortunately happened that he being a middle-aged gentleman, he was not very inquisitive, and my messmates being advanced in years, and not so active as young people, did not tumble me about or undress me.
>
> The pain in my head was so exceeding bad that I was almost deprived of my sense, yet notwithstanding my pain, I had a continual fear upon me of being found out, and as I lay in my hammock I was always listening to hear what they said, or whether they had made any discovery. My apprehensions were soon removed, on finding they were as ignorant as before with respect to that particular, so then I continued in my hammock very easy and satisfied.

In addition to her head wound, Lacy was suffering from scurvy, for although the *Royal Sovereign* while stationed in a home port was supposed to be issued supplementary provisions of fresh meat and vegetables, not enough were provided to prevent the terrible disease from attacking the crew.

Once again Lacy was befriended by a bumboat woman:

> Her kindness was the more acceptable as my teeth were grown so loose in my head that I could not eat anything, but by the care of this woman I wanted for nothing and in a short time found myself so much recovered that I could go to the doctor and have my head dressed every day.

Lacy now joined a new mess and became friendly with one of her messmates, the captain of the forecastle, "whose name was Philip M——t——n, who had a notable woman to his wife":

> They were worth money, and lived very happy together on board the ship; and indeed few in our circumstances lived so comfortably as we did. This woman used to wash for me, and also for impressed men as they came on board.

Anyone with spare cash seemed rich to Lacy, even a woman who took in washing.

> And if I did any work for these pressed men, my messmates would tell them they must pay for it, because I had no friend in the world to help me;…one would give me a pair of stockings, another breeches, and the rest would supply me with other necessaries.

Next, the boatswain of the *Royal Sovereign*, Robert Dawkins, who took a fatherly interest in Lacy, asked her into his mess.[25] "He being very kind to me," she wrote, "I lived extremely happy." Dawkins would continue to be a loyal friend and mentor to her throughout her later years in the navy.

Lacy was also gratified that she was able to attend the school on board "to learn to write and cast accompts."[26] Her only discontent was that for a year and nine months she was not once allowed out of the ship although in sight of Portsmouth. Finally, shortly before Christmas 1762 the crew of the *Royal Sovereign* were paid off, and Lacy was dismissed:

> On this occasion, my joy was so great that I ran up and down, scarcely knowing how to contain myself.

Dawkins invited her to stay at his house in Portsmouth "and [to] eat and drink there."

The *Sandwich* had just arrived at Spithead, and the day after Christmas, Lacy went on board to visit Baker. He welcomed her into his cabin and called in her old pal Jeremiah Paine, the gunner's servant. Baker gave them a bottle of wine and a plum pudding and sent them off by themselves "to tell what had happened to each other since our last parting."

Baker was about to leave for his home in Chatham and told Lacy that if she would go with him, he would have her apprenticed at Chatham Dockyard. She did not trust him and decided to rejoin the *Royal Sovereign,* for "the captain of the *Royal Sovereign* kept me upon the books and paid me, which the carpenter never did to this day."

She entered as purser's servant, a position that allowed her to go on shore to run errands for the officers, and she took every opportunity to try to become a shipwright's apprentice at Portsmouth Dockyard. In the spring of 1763, she succeeded.

Lacy's success was quite remarkable. It was especially difficult to get an apprenticeship at that time, when the war had just ended; the Treaty of Paris had been signed on 10 February 1763. But apprenticeships were hard to get at any time. It was not skill that mattered, but influence. Traditionally, an apprenticeship was handed down from father to son. While some experience in carpentry was helpful, it was not required; a shipwright's apprentice needed only to be over the age of sixteen, to be over four feet six inches tall, and to come well recommended.[27]

The boatswain of the *Sandwich* told Lacy that Alexander M'Clean (spelled McLean in the muster books), acting carpenter of the *Royal William,* might take her as his apprentice, and Dawkins encouraged her to apply:

> He advised me to agree to the proposal for that it was better to have some trade than none at all and added, "I know him [M'Clean] to be a good-tempered man, and seven years [the

length of an apprenticeship] is not for ever, so I would have you go."

M'Clean offered her the apprenticeship; she accepted and moved her chest and bedding to the *Royal William,* an eighty-four-gun ship, then in ordinary (out of commission).[28]

> [On the morning of 4 March 1763] my master ordered me to clean myself, and be ready to go ashore with him as he designed to bind me 'prentice that very day.

There was a heavy sea running, and their boat could not get into the regular landing:

> [We] were forced to go to the north jetty, where some caulkers' stages lay alongside, at which place they had driven some nails into the piles (to climb up by)…which were at least sixteen feet high.
> My master and the gunner had got safely up, and were walking on; but when I had almost climbed to the top, letting go the rope to take hold of the ringbolt, my foot slipped, and I fell down into the sea; but as soon as I appeared again, the boys upon the stage soon pulled me up…and I recovered myself as well as I could. Presently…my master and the gunner began to miss me; and coming back to see where I was (observing me on the stage) asked the reason why I had been so long in coming…. I then told them that I had fell overboard. On which my master laughed, and sent me to a blacksmith's shop, where I immediately pulled off my coat and waistcoat to dry myself; after which he [M'Clean]…brought me out of the yard and gave me something hot to drink, to wet the inside; for the outside was sufficiently soaked before.
> My master and I went together to wait on the builder to know if he approved of me for an apprentice…. "Why," said the builder, "I like him very well, for I think he is a stout lad."
> So my master had me entered, but not as a yard servant as he was not allowed to, being only carpenter of the *Deptford,* a

fourth-rate man-of-war. At this time he did duty on board the
Royal William [a second-rate ship], the carpenter of which was
dead, and he [M'Clean] had some hopes of procuring the place
for himself.

M'Clean arranged to have Lacy work under a Mr. Dunn, a quar-
terman (shipwright and foreman) at the yard.

> Mr. Dunn put me under one Mr. Cote to learn my business, who
> was a very good-tempered man and took great pains to instruct
> me; he liked me very well and seemed to be greatly delighted to
> hear me talk.... This affair being thus concluded, my master
> went and bought me a saw, an ax, and a chisel, which made me
> very proud.
>   I was [now] a cadet [assigned] to work one week in the yard
> and another on board a new ship, the *Britannia,* just launched.

M'Clean was a gentle, patient master, but like Baker before him,
he was a heavy drinker and was constantly in debt, and since the
pay of apprentices, like the pay of ship's servants, went to their masters, Lacy never saw any of her wages and had to scramble for
spending money:

> When we went to work on board the *Niger* frigate..., the quar-
> terman, a person whom I worked with, was very kind to me. I
> had my provisions of the king [a daily food ration], so we made
> one allowance serve us and sold the other to the purser for a
> guinea a quarter.... And when I worked in the dockyard, I used
> to sell my [wood] chips at the gate, and sometimes would carry
> the bundle to Mr. Dawkins, and was welcome to his house
> whenever I pleased.

Shipwrights and their apprentices were allowed to sell their wood
shavings to the townspeople, who used them for kindling.
  M'Clean and his mistress, a boisterous woman who lived with
him on board the *Royal William,* gave many wild parties together

with a Mr. Robinson, his wife, and "a deputy purser's wife." (The women had all grown up together in the town of Gosport, across the water from Portsmouth.) Lacy was required to act as servant at these parties, a tiresome task after a twelve-hour day at the dockyard, but she had great stamina, and she enjoyed the attention the women paid her:

> They sent me for liquor and would often get as drunk as David's sow, and in the height of these frolics, they would say about me, "Aye, he is, aye, he is, the best boy on board."
>
> In regard to Mother Robinson, I must acknowledge, she would do any kind office for me. Indeed, I was in general well beloved by the women if by nobody else; and, thank God, greatly respected by my master, so that I lived a quite happy life; and went to work at the yard every day.

When M'Clean sent Lacy to fetch beer on shore, she borrowed the boatswain's canoe and soon learned to handle it well. One evening her master challenged Lacy to race the canoe against him and three other men in a four-oared boat. He promised to give her a sixpence if she beat them. She won with ease:

> I fell a-laughing at them and called out, "Where's my money, where's my money!" He told me I should have it, but instead of giving it me, he took us all on shore and spent it among us.

She was shocked when she learned that M'Clean's mistress was not his wife but the wife of another seaman, then at Greenwich Hospital. Lacy did not, however, let her disapproval affect her friendly relationship with the woman:

> My master frequently asked me to dine with him on Sunday if they had any company on board, and then I got a sufficiency [of food], for he would always have me to wait at table. While I was laying the cloth, my mistress would stroke me down the face and say I was a clever fellow. Which expression made me blush.

Frequently after supper my master would ask me to favor them with a song.... Wherefore to divert them I commonly sung them two or three songs, which made them merry until about twelve o'clock, when my master would order me with three more boys to row them to the Hard [the shingle beach at Portsmouth Dockyard backed by a street of taverns], after which they made us a present to buy a little beer, but we made all the haste back [to the ship] we could. [The apprentices were due at the dockyard at six the following morning.]

Getting home to the *Royal William* from the dockyard was arduous, especially in winter. Lacy left the yard at 6:00 P.M. and then had a two-mile walk to the pier, where she had to shout across the water for a boat from the *Royal William* to come pick her up:

When the wind was in the east, they could not hear me. Therefore, I was often obliged to stand in the wind and cold until I was almost froze to death, which made me think how happy I would be if my master had a house, for then I should have a good fire to sit by and victuals to eat till the boat came for me....

I shall next proceed to relate what passed concerning the young woman who lived at Mr. Dawkins's house, which place I often went to. Being there one evening, he asked me to stay till morning, as he himself was to remain on board all night; and moreover, the maid insisted on my promising to stay there. Having consented, we sat at cards till twelve o'clock, when some young women who spent the evening with us went home. I then asked the maid where I was to lie. She answered there was no place but with her or her mistress. I told her I would lie in her bed. Accordingly she lighted me up to her chamber. Perceiving her forwardness I thought it was no wonder the young men took such liberties with the other sex when they gave them such encouragement; and I am compelled, for the sake of truth, to say this much of the women; but am far from condemning all for the faults of one or two. However, when a young woman allows too much freedom, it induces the men to think they are all alike.

I must confess that if I had been a young man I could not have withstood the temptations which this young person laid in my way, for she was so fond of me that I was ever at her tongue's end; which was the reason her master and mistress watched her so narrowly. In short, there was nothing I could ask that she would refuse; and, to make me the more sensible of it, my shirts were washed and prepared for me in the very best manner she was able.

At this point M'Clean must have received some of his back wages, for to Lacy's delight, he was able to rent a house on shore. There Lacy and another apprentice, John Lyons, shared a bed in a room on the upper floor. At first Lacy worried that Lyons would discover that she was a woman, but he had less energy than she and went to bed "as soon as he came home from dock…[and] was no sooner abed but asleep."

Kindly M'Clean, with a bit of extra cash, told Lacy, "I should have a new suit of clothes and not go so shabby as I was":

The tailor came as he was directed, and my master gave me my choice of the color, for which I thanked him and fixed upon a blue which he seemed well pleased with; and I was not a little proud to think that I should have good and decent apparel to appear in, as I could then walk out on Sundays with the young women.

Lacy and her friend Edward Turner, who was living in the *Royal William,* had been flirting with a group of friendly young women whom Lacy had met when they came to the dockyard to collect chips. Turner invited Lacy to a party in their honor:

We had a leg of mutton and turnips and a fine plum pudding provided, with plenty of gin and strong beer, which I considered as a grand entertainment for me and the young ladies.… We were very merry with our new acquaintances, and I soon found that Vobbleton Street was the place of their residence.

It was only when Turner and Lacy saw the girls home that Lacy realized that this "couple of merry girls" were not the innocents she had supposed:

> This street in Portsmouth town is inhabited with divers classes of people, so that I soon found what sort of company I was in.

One evening when M'Clean was away, his mistress returned home from a drunken evening in Gosport and brought with her a group of revelers, including a waterman—the one, perhaps, who brought the group back across the harbor. (A waterman was the equivalent of today's taxi driver, only his taxi was a boat.) Upon their arrival she hailed Lacy, who had retired to her bed upstairs:

> She soon called me and I told her I was coming down; which I did without the knowledge of my bedfellow.... I found that she wanted some beer, for she said she was thirsty. Accordingly, I went and brought a pot of ringwood [a kind of ale], and, it being summertime, she sat at the door to drink it, over against which there being a wheelbarrow, I went and sat down upon it. My mistress observing me, came and placed herself in my lap, stroking me down the face, telling the waterman what she would do for me, so that the people present could not forbear laughing to see her sit in such a young boy's lap as she thought I was. However, she had not been long in this situation before my master came home, and passed by her as she sat there; but taking no notice that he saw us, went in doors.
>
> And indeed I was very much frightened lest he should beat me, but I thought he could not justly be angry with me, for it was all her own fault.
>
> I went then to try the door to discover if my master had locked it.... I told her the door was locked and that we must both lie in the street. Upon which she said she would go back to Gosport, and that I should go along with her.
>
> As we were thus talking together under the window, my master, overhearing her say she would set off for Gosport,...threw up the window and soused us all over with a chamber pot full of

water, which made me fall into such a fit of laughter that my
sides were ready to burst…to see what a pickle she was in.

While the woman was mopping herself off, Lacy tried the door
again and, finding it was not locked after all, slipped into the house:

> I immediately took off my shoes and stockings, ran upstairs,
> pulled my bedfellow out of his place, and got into it myself; for
> I supposed if my master came up to thrash me, he would lay
> hold of my bedfellow first, and then I should have time to get
> away. However, as good luck would have it, he did not concern
> himself with me but vented his anger on my mistress when she
> came in, telling her she might go to the waterman again, and
> would not let her come to bed.
>
> In the morning my bedfellow John Lyons wondered how he
> came into my place in the bed, for he had heard nothing about
> the matter, being such a sound sleeper. We both went as usual to
> work at the dock.

Not long after this incident, M'Clean was arrested as a debtor and
carried off to the jail at Winchester. Lacy was greatly upset to hear
of her poor master's arrest, and twice she went all the way to
Winchester to visit him. The first time, she walked there and back.
M'Clean's mistress was less grieved:

> [She] began stripping the house and carrying the furniture to
> the pawnbroker's, which indeed was the only method that could
> be taken to procure us some victuals.… My mistress seldom lay
> at home above a night in the week and went abroad in the
> morning, so that for the remaining part of the week, when I
> came home from work at night, [I] was obliged to go from house
> to house [to get food] as it were in my master's name.

M'Clean's mistress, despite her straitened finances, found enough
money to continue to carouse, and sometimes she inveigled Lacy
into going with her "to Gosport into those lewd houses in South
Street, where I was obliged to be very free with the girls." One night

Lacy's mistress took her to the theater together with "a young woman called Sarah How, who indeed was a very handsome girl":

> From that time the above Sarah How became very free and intimate with me; nor did I ever go to town without calling to see her, when we walked out together.

After several months of imprisonment, M'Clean was released under an arrangement that required him to pay over all his assets, including his apprentices, to his debtors. He was also obliged to go to sea, where he was less likely to run up more debts. He turned Lacy over to a Mr. Aulquier, who was continuously drunk and brawling with his wife. M'Clean then joined the *Africa* and disappeared from Lacy's life. He left in 1765, and for the remaining five and a half years of her apprenticeship, Lacy was passed from one drunken, debt-ridden master to another:

> I had not been long with him [Aulquier] before he turned me over to another man to pay his debts, and when I had worked that out, was again turned over to a third, so that being shifted from one to another, I had neither clothes to my back nor shoes or stockings to my feet. I was frequently, even in the dead of winter, obliged to go to the dockyard barefooted.

Throughout this period Lacy's one comfort was that she continued to prove a great success with the ladies. "On Shrove Tuesday in the year 1766," Betsy, a former girlfriend, asked her to a dance. Lacy accepted, although Dawkins had warned her that Miss Betsy was not a proper young lady. After the party, however, fearing that Dawkins would hear that she had renewed this unsuitable acquaintanceship, Lacy decided that she would not see Betsy again. But her resolve did not last long:

> One day, as I was going down the Common in Union Street, she [Betsy] happened to stand at a door; and seeing me, said, "Will, I thought you was dead."

"Why so?" returned I. "Did you send anybody to kill me?"

"No," replied she, "but I thought I should never see you any more."

"Well," said I, "you are welcome to think so still, if you please, but I must be going."

"What!" said she. "You are in a great hurry now to be gone; if you was along with that Gosport girl you would not be in such haste to leave her."

I said, "I am not in such a hurry to be gone from your company, Betsy; what makes you think so?"

After this little chat, though with some seeming reserve on both sides, she asked if I would come in. I went in and sat down, and then asked her if she would come next Sunday to Gosport and drink tea. She told me she would. Thus it was all made up again.

Lacy continued to see Betsy until Dawkins learned of the affair and questioned her about it. "William," he said, "I am sorry you will walk out with her when I have told you what she is." Lacy staunchly denied everything:

"Well, sir," said I, "I am much obliged to you for your advice, but as for keeping her company, I do not; nor do I know that I shall ever speak to her again."

This matter passed over for some time, and by giving attention to my work I thought little or nothing about things of this kind. However, one evening my fellow servant Sarah Chase began talking as we were sitting together about sweethearts and said to me in a joking manner, "I think you have lost your intended."

"Well," replied I, "I must be content."

She said, "There are more in the world to be had."

"Aye," replied I, "when one is gone, another will come."

"For my part," added she, "I have got never a one."

"Well," said I, "suppose you and I were to keep company together?"

"You and I," answered she, "will consider of it."

From that time on, Lacy and Sarah Chase saw a great deal of one another:

> I had not yet served quite three years of my time; nevertheless, it was agreed that neither of us should walk out with any other person without the mutual consent of each other. Notwithstanding this agreement, if she saw me talking to any young woman, she was immediately fired with jealousy and could scarce command her temper. This I did sometimes to try her. However, we were very intimate together.
>
> And to give me a farther proof of her affection, she would frequently come down to the place where the boat landed [to bring the dockworkers from their ships] to see me, which made the people believe we should soon be married. One man observed, "Well done, Chandler, you come on very well." Another said that I should be a cuckold before I had long been married for that she was too large for me, as I should make but a little man.

Lacy was fond of Sarah but could not resist flirting with other young women:

> Sarah began to have a very suspicious opinion of me, on observing I spoke to another girl, for one evening when I went indoors to ask her for some supper, she looked at me with a countenance that bespoke a mixture of jealousy and anger. It then came into my mind that there would soon be terrible work. Whereupon I asked what was the matter with her. She told me to go to the squint-eyed girl and inquire the matter there. "Very well," said I, "so I can."
>
> From hence I soon knew what was the ground of all. It seems the taphouse woman had been telling her more of this affair at large, which brought me into a great difficulty; and indeed I lived a very disagreeable life at home, especially since I could not get my victuals as before.

Sarah soon forgave Lacy, and they continued their courtship.

In 1767 Lacy got leave to visit her parents and sailed in a naval vessel to the Downs, then traveled overland to Ash. She was now twenty-seven and had not been home since running away at nineteen:

> I found all the family very well; and took that opportunity of satisfying their earnest expectations by recounting the various turns of fortune I had met with and gone through during an absence of almost eight years.

Lacy does not mention their feelings about her living as a man. She apparently maintained her male role in public during the visit, so that only the family and a few close friends knew who the visiting sailor really was.

There is an interjection here that harks back to Lacy's teenage infatuation with her dancing partner:

> The young man on whose account I at first left my parents had frequently caused inquiry to be made when I was to come home, expressing a great desire to see me, but I had no inclination to receive any visits from him.

Why he should want to see her at this point when he had expressed no special interest in her when they had met eight years earlier is not explained.

Not long after Lacy returned to Portsmouth, a frightening episode occurred. A Mrs. Low, a close friend of the Lacy family in Ash who knew Mary's secret, moved to Portsmouth, and although she had promised never to reveal Lacy's true identity, she spread the rumor to anyone who would listen that William Chandler was a woman. Lacy, however, had no inkling of her perfidy:

> [One morning when] I went to the dock it was whispered about that I was a woman, which threw me into a most terrible fright, believing that some of the boys were going to search me. It was now much about breakfast time when, coming on shore in order to go to my chest for my breakfast, two men of our company called and said they wanted to speak to me. I went to them.

"Mary Lacy's sex discovered by the workmen in Portsmouth Dockyard after she had worked in the yard and served at sea eleven years disguised as a man." From *The Female Shipwright; or, Life and Extraordinary Adventures of Mayr* [sic] *Lacy... Written by Herself* (Philadelphia: William M'Carty, 1814), frontispiece. COURTESY OF THE TRUSTEES OF THE BOSTON PUBLIC LIBRARY

"What think you, Chandler," one of them said. "The people will have it that you are a woman!" Which struck me with such a panic that I knew not what to say. However, I had the presence of mind to laugh it off, as if it was not worth notice.

On going to my chest again, I perceived several apprentices waiting who wanted to search me, but I took care not to run lest that should increase their suspicion. Hereupon one Mr. Penny of our company came up and asked them what they meant by surrounding me in that manner, telling them at the same time that the first person that offered to touch me would not only be drubbed by him, but [that he] would carry him before the builder afterwards, which made them all sheer off....

However, when I had done work, the man whose name was Corbin and his mate who taught me my business came and told me in a serious manner that I must go with them to be searched. "For if you don't," said they, "you will be overhauled by the boys."

Indeed, I knew not what to do in this case, but I considered that they were very sober men, and that it was safer to trust them than expose myself to the rudeness of the boys. They put the question very seriously, which I as ingenuously answered, though it made me cry so that I could scarce speak, at which declaration of mine in plainly telling them that I was a woman, they seemed greatly surprised and offered to take their oaths of secrecy.

When they went back, the people asked them if it was true what they had heard.

"No," said they, "he is a man-and-a-half to a great many."

"Aye," said one, "I thought Chandler could not be so great with his mistress if he was not a man. I'm sure she would not have brought him to the point if he was not so."

And another said, "I'm sure he's no girl; if he was, he would not have gone after so many [women] for nothing and would have soon been found out."

For such talk as this among the men, in a day or two the matter quite dropped; yet now and then they would say, "I wonder how it should come into the heads of the people to think that Chandler was a girl; I am sure there is not the least appearance of it in the make or shape of him."...

My girl at Gosport [Sarah Chase] had heard it, but could not believe it.

Several years passed before Lacy discovered that it was Mrs. Low who had betrayed her, and by that time she was lodging at Mrs. Low's house "in the Tree Rope Walk, on Portsmouth Common":

As soon as I heard that Mrs. Low had told everybody who I was, I was ready to break my heart.... I thought she was the best friend I had.... Indeed, I esteemed myself happy in having met a person I could freely unbosom myself to.

Lacy not only had to find a new place to live, but from that time onward she was also tortured by fears that her gender would be discovered.

In the spring of 1770 Mary Lacy received her certificate as a shipwright:

> On the last day before my time expired, being at work upon the *Pallas* frigate, Sarah came and invited me to breakfast with her the next morning, which I did. Having afterwards cleaned myself, I went to the builder's office and told him it was the last day of my time and hoped he had no objection against my certificate's being allowed me.... He then called his clerk and ordered him to prepare a certificate, which he accordingly did; after which I went to each of the proper persons, who readily signed it. I then carried the certificate to the Clerk of the Cheque's office, where I was entered as a man.

She had at last acquired the respected position she had worked toward for seven years; she was free from cruel masters, and she actually received a living wage, although the navy was slow to pay.[29] Tragically, however, she was to have little time to enjoy her new status.

After a major fire in the dockyard on 27 July 1770—Lacy gives the date as 16 May—all the yard workers were required to work overtime; they worked as much as five hours in addition to their twelve-hour day, and the strain caused Lacy's rheumatism to return.[30] The anguished way she writes about her battle against her illness reveals how desperate she was to maintain her role as a shipwright:

> [When the overtime hours were reduced] I was not sorry...as I was almost spent with working so close, for in a little time afterwards I was seized with so bad a swelling in my thighs that I was not able to walk, and was unwilling the doctor should look at it lest he should find me out. I therefore sent for the quarterman to answer for me that I was sick, which he accordingly did,

and I continued a week before I was able to go into the yard
again and was then incapable of doing any work.

When Lacy recovered from this attack she was ordered to work
in various ships anchored at Spithead, where she had to stay on
board day and night:

> We were in as bad a situation as before, having no other place to
> lie but the softest plank we could find; so that such a wretched
> accommodation during that time made me catch cold again in
> my thighs and occasioned my illness to return. However, I soon
> mended....
>
> A short time after this I was, on account of lameness, forced
> to go upon the doctor's list for a fortnight, but thank God I got
> the better of this and went to work again, though continually
> apprehensive of being surprised unawares, for I did not know
> the particular persons my false friend had betrayed me to.
>
> Soon afterwards our company was ordered to tear up an old
> forty-gun ship, which was so very difficult to take to pieces that
> I strained my loins in the attempt, the effects of which I felt very
> sensibly at night when I went home, for I could hardly stand and
> had no appetite to my victuals. But notwithstanding my legs
> would scarce support me, I continued working till the ship was
> quite demolished, and then we were ordered on board the *Sand-
> wich* to bring on her waling [timbers bolted to the sides of a
> ship], which was very heavy.
>
> This increased my weakness to such a degree that the going
> to work proved very irksome to me, insomuch that everybody
> wondered what was the matter.
>
> However, I still continued my labor till want of strength
> obliged me to quit it. And then I went to the doctor's shop and
> told him I had strained my loins, which disabled me from
> working. Whereupon he gave me something which he thought
> would relieve me. I took it, but had it not been for the infinite
> mercy of God toward me, I should certainly have been killed by
> it, the medicine being altogether improper for my complaint.

In consequence whereof, instead of growing better I became every day worse than the former, which made me think I could not live long.

However, in process of time my complaint abated, but not so as to enable me to work as I had done before, nor could I carry the same burthens as usual, which made me very uneasy.

Lacy slowly accepted the fact that she was going to have to resign from the dockyard:

While I continued in this weak condition, I imagined that if I could go down to Kent [to her home in Ash] I might get a friend to help me out of the [dock]yard, but getting somewhat better, I went to work as well as I could.

The loss of my father and mother likewise greatly aggravated my concern, and I began to think of endeavoring to obtain liberty of the builder to go into Kent for a fortnight, which he readily granted.

Lacy gives no details of her parents' deaths. It is sad that they died just when she could at last expect their approval of her status and when she could send some money home. In the past she had always ended her letters to them "Your undutiful daughter," but a letter she wrote soon after she became a shipwright was signed "Your dutiful daughter."

She got leave to go to Ash, where she hoped to get help from family friends in arranging for a disability pension from the navy, and a Mrs. Deverton contacted her brother Mr. Richardson in London, asking him to aid Lacy in petitioning the Admiralty, whose offices were in London. Richardson—who had known Lacy's family for some years and was apparently aware that Lacy was a woman—was a man of some prominence, perhaps a solicitor:

He sent me word he could not do anything for me at that time because all the gentlemen [at the Admiralty?] were out of town, but that in a month's time he would write and let me know further.

Lacy returned to work "but was in a short time after taken as ill as ever."

Toward the close of the year 1771, Richardson invited Lacy to come stay with him and his wife at their house in Kensington, just west of London, while he helped her through the lengthy procedure of applying for a pension:

> This news in a few days gave a happy turn to my disorder and almost restored me to health, so that I embraced the first opportunity of going over to Gosport to take leave of them all [her various girlfriends] and [then] went directly home to make myself ready to go with the coach [to London].
>
> My parting with the young women occasioned a scene of great perplexity and distress; and indeed one of them was ready to break her heart. This was poor Sarah, whose pitiable case affected me very much. However, I set off from Portsmouth the second day of December 1771 and reached Kensington the next day.

The complicated process of petitioning for a pension could take months, and it was not always successful, even for those with the severest need. It may have been Richardson who suggested that Lacy apply under her own name, and probably because the case of a woman petitioner caught the attention of the lords of the Admiralty, the pension was granted within two months. On Tuesday, 28 January 1772, the Admiralty minutes report:

> A Petition was read from Mary Lacey [*sic*] setting forth that in the Year 1759 she disguised herself in Men's Cloaths and enter'd on board His Maj^ts Fleet, where having served til the end of the War, she bound herself apprentice to the Carpenter of the *Royal William* and having served Seven Years, then enter'd as a Shipwright in Portsmouth Yard where she has continued ever since; but that finding her health and constitution impaired by

so laborious an Employment, she is obliged to give it up for the future, and therefore, praying some Allowance for her Support during the remainder of her life:

Resolved, in consideration of the particular Circumstances attending this Woman's case, the truth of which has been attested by the Commissioner of the Yard at Portsmouth, that she be allowed a Pension equal to that granted to Superannuated Shipwrights.[31]

The Navy Board's Abstract of Letters gives the same information, except that it states that "she was commonly called Mrs. Chandler."[32] She was granted twenty pounds a year.

The last two paragraphs of Lacy's book introduce a most surprising event: her marriage to a certain Mr. Slade. These paragraphs seem to be tacked on to her narrative in order to give it a storybook ending: and so they were married and lived happily ever after. It also reassures the reader that, when all is said and done, Mary Lacy was heterosexual:

After the lords of the Admiralty had granted my superannuated pension, I continued with Mr. Richardson at Kensington for about the space of ten months. During which time, on going to Deptford [a dockyard down the Thames from London] to receive my money, I was met by one Mr. Slade, who had removed thither from Portsmouth Yard by order of the board. He had not seen me before in women's apparel; yet having heard of my metamorphosis, he inquired kindly after my health and offered his services to conduct me back to Kensington.

On the road thither, he expressed a great affection for me; and at the same time requested me to give him my hand at the altar, allowing me a proper time to consider of his offer. Though I had repeatedly declared that I would remain single, yet afterward, having the utmost reason to believe that there subsisted a real and mutual affection betwixt us, and that the hand of Providence was engaged in bringing about our union, I at length gave my consent; in consequence of which we were married and now enjoy the utmost happiness the state affords; which I have the most sanguine hopes of a continuance of, since my husband is not only sober and industrious, but having been convinced, ever since the year 1762, of the important truths of Christianity, his conduct towards mankind in general, founded on a love of virtue, is upright and exemplary; at the same time that in his conjugal relations he behaves in the most endearing and indulgent manner. Thus united, I have, by the blessing of God, attained more than a bare chance for happiness in my present state, and have also the most solid grounds to look for the permanent enjoyment of it in future.

Thus ends the autobiography.

Before discussing the marriage, I would like to point out that the autobiography includes a list of 104 subscribers who presumably covered the publication costs. Only a few of the names in the list appear in the autobiography, but among those is Richard Baker, Lacy's master in the *Sandwich*. William Chandler's metamorphosis into a woman must have come as a great shock to this old sailor who had never suspected the truth. And it is remarkable that the grudging, parsimonious Baker was willing to support the publishing venture. Perhaps at the time that he became a subscriber he was not aware of the contents of the book. Whether he actually paid over any money is doubtful.

In regard to Lacy's marriage to Mr. Slade, it seems possible that it never took place, and it is even questionable that this Mr. Slade existed. Throughout the autobiography Lacy is chatty about other important events in her life, but she offers no details about either the wedding or the bridegroom, except for assuring the reader of her husband's Christian virtue and endearing conjugal behavior.

Of course, it is possible that Lacy, at the age of thirty-three, after twelve years of living as a man, reverted to the restricted life of a woman, and a married woman at that. The preface is signed

"M. Slade, Deptford, July 7, 1773," and the title page notes, "Printed and sold by M. Lewis at No. 1, S. Bladon, No. 28, in Pater-noster Row, and by the Author in King-street, Deptford." This indicates that Lacy was living in Deptford at the time the book was published, but it does not prove that she was married to Slade.[33] I even wonder if she picked up the name of her husband from Sir Thomas Slade, the famous master shipwright (naval architect) and surveyor of the navy from 1755 to 1771. He designed the *Sandwich* and was responsible for much of the planning for the rebuilding of Portsmouth Dockyard after the fire of 1770, which means that Lacy would have been particularly aware of his name at the time of her retirement in 1771.[34]

In a society in which a married woman was completely under the control of her husband, socially and financially, it is difficult to picture the extraordinarily independent and strong-willed Lacy as the dutiful wife of an "upright and exemplary husband." If she did invent this husband, it was not the first time she had lied with alacrity. She had, for example, flatly denied to her friend Dawkins that she was going out with the immoral Betsy.

Lacy so much enjoyed her life as a man, despite the difficulties she had to cope with, that it would be a more joyful prospect to suppose that she continued in a male role after leaving the navy. Once she was free from long hours of work in the damp holds of ships, her rheumatism may have been allayed, and perhaps she found work as a house carpenter.

One thing seems certain. In whatever situation she found herself, Mary Lacy continued to meet each new adventure head-on, as she had always done.

NOTES

Sources from the Public Record Office, Kew, London, are cited using the following abbreviations:

ADM = Admiralty Records in the Public Record Office
 ADM 1 class, in-letters of the Admiralty Board
  ADM 1/5253–5474, 1680–1839, Admiralty minutes of evidence and verdicts in court-martial, returned by the judge-advocate in each case
 ADM 2 class, out-letters of the Admiralty
 ADM 36 and 37, ships' muster books
 ADM 42, muster books for ships in ordinary (not in commission)
 ADM 82, Chatham Chest Records; later became Greenwich Hospital Records
 ADM 102, naval hospital musters, 1740–1860
WO = War Office documents in the Public Record Office
 WO 116 class, Chelsea Hospital Out-pension Admission Books, 1715–1882

Most of the following references to Admiralty Records are to ships' muster books (ADM 36, 37, and 42). It is remarkable how many of these eighteenth- and early-nineteenth-century musters have been preserved, considering the fortunes of war, the erosions of time, and the Blitz. While it is pleasurable to work with the actual muster books, the pleasure is mixed with anxiety, for the musters are often out of sequence and the names are listed, not alphabetically, but in the random order in which the men lined up on deck for the lieutenant to list them. There are hundreds of entries, written carelessly in an obsolete style of handwriting; abbreviations are used, and the ink is faded. But what a thrill when, after combing seemingly endless columns, one finds the searched-for name.

Introduction

Epigraph from John Masefield, ed., *A Sailor's Garland*, 2d ed. (London: Methuen, 1908), 292–93.

1. Julia Llewellyn Smith, "All the Nice Girls Now Are Sailors," *Times* (London), 2 November 1993. To *splice* (repair) *the main brace* was the traditional naval term for issuing the crew an extra ration of rum or grog in bad weather or after they had performed an especially arduous task. The main brace was attached to the lower yard of the mainmast and was hauled to bring the ship around to the wind—a difficult job.

2. In regard to the term *female tars,* used in the title of this book, *tar,* or *Jack Tar,* was a nickname for naval seamen. It probably derived from their use of tar to slick down their pigtails and to coat their outer garments against wet weather.

CHAPTER 1
Prostitutes and Seamen's Wives on Board in Port

Epigraph from George G. Carey, ed., *A Sailor's Songbag: An American Rebel in an English Prison, 1777–1779* (Amherst: University of Massachusetts Press, 1976), 147.

1. Sir John Mennes to Samuel Pepys, 19 April 1666, *Calendar of State Papers Domestic (1665–1666),* quoted in J. J. Keevil, Christopher Lloyd, and J. L. S. Coulter, *Medicine and the Navy, 1200–1900,* 4 vols., vols. 1 and 2 by Keevil, vols. 3 and 4 by Lloyd and Coulter (Edinburgh: E. and S. Livingstone, 1957–63), 2:91.

2. *The Diary of Henry Teonge, Chaplain on Board H.M.'s Ships* Assistance, Bristol, *and* Royal Oak, *Anno 1675–1679,* ed. G. E. Manwaring (London: George Routledge and Sons, 1927), 29.

3. William Robinson, *Nautical Economy* (London: William Robinson, 1836), reprinted as *Jack Nastyface: Memoirs of a Seaman* (Annapolis: Naval Institute Press, 1973), 87–92.

4. *Memoirs of Admiral the Right Honourable, the Earl of St. Vincent* [John Jervis], ed. Jedidiah Stephens Tucker, 2 vols. (London: Richard Bentley, 1844), 2:120.

5. [Edward Hawker], *Statement Respecting the Prevalence of Certain Immoral Practices Prevailing in His Majesty's Navy* (London: Ellerton and Henderson, 1821), 3–5.

6. Bumboats were round-bottomed oared boats, privately owned, that brought produce and other items out to the ships in harbor. The derivation of the word *bumboat* is obscure. It may come from the Dutch word *boomboot,* a similarly shaped fishing boat. The nineteenth-century naval historian William Laird Clowes suggested that the name derived from *bum,* the buttocks, because of the boat's clumsy shape. William Laird Clowes, *The Royal Navy: A History from the Earliest Times to the Present,* 7 vols. (London: Sampson Low, Marston, 1897–1903), vol. 5, *1803-1815,* 26 n.

7. See Suzanne J. Stark, "Sailors' Pets in the Royal Navy in the Age of Sail," *American Neptune* 51 (Spring 1991): 77–82.

8. James Anthony Gardner, *Above and under Hatches,* ed. Christopher Lloyd (London: Batchworth, 1955), 27.

9. William Richardson, *A Mariner of England: An Account of the Career of William Richardson...[1780–1819] as Told by Himself,* ed. Spencer Childers (London: Conway Maritime Press, 1970), 225–26.

10. Ibid., 226.

11. Edward Thompson, *A Sailor's Letters, Written to His Select Friends in England during His Voyages and Travels in Europe, Asia, Africa, and America from 1754 to 1759,* 2 vols., 2d ed. (London: T. Becket, 1767), 2:24–25.

12. "Captain's Orders, No. 21, *Andromeda* at Sea, August 1, 1788," quoted in *Letters and Papers of Admiral of the Fleet, Sir Thomas Byam Martin,* ed. Richard Vesey Hamilton, 3 vols. (London: Navy Records Society, 1903), appendix A, 1:347.

13. *A Seaman's Life on Board a Man-of-War* (Portsmouth: Griffin and Co., c. 1881), 5–6.

14. Linda McKee (Maloney), "Mad Jack and the Missionaries," *American Heritage* 22 (April 1971): 35–36; David F. Long, *"Mad Jack": The Biography of Captain John Percival, USN, 1779–1862* (Westport, Conn.: Greenwood, 1993), 67–72.

15. N. A. M. Rodger denies that the Georgian navy "was a floating concentration camp," but his contention that leave was regularly granted is based on specific instances when officers did give leave. These exceptions do not prove the rule. Rodger does not account for seamen's recurring complaints over lack of leave, nor does he explain why, if adequate leave was given, the navy allowed hundreds of prostitutes to come on board its ships. See N. A. M. Rodger, *The Wooden World: An Anatomy of the Georgian Navy* (Annapolis: Naval Institute Press, 1986), 143–44.

16. James Boswell, *Life of Johnson*, ed. George Birkbeck Hill, 6 vols. (Oxford: Clarendon, 1934), 1:348. Johnson reiterated the idea several times. See 2:438, 5:514.

17. Michael Oppenheim, *History of the Administration of the Royal Navy from Early Times through 1661 and of Merchant Shipping in Relation to the Navy* (London: John Lane, Bodley Head, 1896), vol. 1, *1509–1661*, 318.

18. Christopher Lloyd, *The British Seaman, 1200–1860: A Social Survey* (Rutherford, N.J.: Fairleigh Dickinson University Press, 1970), 245.

19. See Michael Lewis, *A Social History of the Navy, 1793–1815* (London: George Allen and Unwin, 1960), 419–21, 442, 413.

20. Lloyd, *British Seaman*, 258–64. Smallpox vaccination did not become compulsory until 1864.

21. Admiral Cuthbert Collingwood, recalling the time in 1780 when he was captain of the twenty-eight-gun frigate *Hinchinbroke* at San Juan, wrote, "I survived most of my ship's company, having buried in four months 180 of the 200 who composed it. Mine was not a singular case for every ship that was long there suffered to the same degree. The transports' men all died, and some of the ships, having none left to take care of them, sunk in the harbour." *A Selection from the Public and Private Correspondence of Vice-Admiral Lord [Cuthbert] Collingwood*, ed. G. L. Newnham Collingwood, 2 vols., 5th ed. (London: James Ridgway, 1837), 1:10. See also Lloyd and Coulter, *Medicine and the Navy*, 3:171–72.

22. Between 1653 and 1797 an able seaman earned twenty-four shillings a month; an ordinary seaman, nineteen shillings; and a landman (after that rating was established), eighteen shillings. Deductions amounted to almost two shillings. These wages were less than merchant crews earned—a great deal less in wartime, when men in privateers often made excellent money and regular cargo vessels were competing with the privateers for men. Even soldiers earned more, although their expenses were higher: in 1797 a common soldier was paid thirty shillings a month. By 1806 an able seaman earned 33s. 6d.; an ordinary seaman, 25s. 6d.; and a landman, 22s. 6d. Even with inflation this was an improvement, but pay was still late in coming. See Lloyd, *British Seaman*, 248–50; Rodger, *Wooden World*, 125; and Brian Lavery, *Nelson's Navy: The Ships, Men, and Organization, 1793–1815* (London: Conway Maritime Press, 1989), 130.

23. Thomas Cochrane, *The Autobiography of a Seaman*, ed. Douglas Cochrane (London: Richard Bentley and Son, 1890), 322–23.

24. W. Senior, "The Navy as Penitentiary," *Mariner's Mirror* 16 (1930): 313–14.

25. See Lewis, *Social History*, 127–33, and Lloyd, *British Seaman*, 122, 158–59, 213–19.

26. See Rodger, *Wooden World*, 159–61.

27. Beer supplemented or replaced water, which was usually foul. The rum ration was served morning and evening in the form of grog (rum mixed with water, and later lime or lemon juice). The half-pint rum ration was halved in 1824 and halved again in 1850. It was discontinued in 1970. See James Pack, *Nelson's Blood* (Annapolis: Naval Institute Press, 1983).

28. Charles Vinicombe Penrose, *Observations on Corporal Punishment* (London: Bodmin, 1824), 51–65, quoted in Eugene L. Rasor, *Reform in the Royal Navy: A Social History of the Lower Deck, 1850 to 1880* (Hamden, Conn.: Shoe String Press, Archon Books, 1976), 97.

29. "A Booke of Orders for the Warre both by sea and land written by Thomas Audley at the Comand of King Henry the viij," Harleian Collection, British Library. The quotation comes from the section "Orders to be used in the Kinges majestes navie by the see," which is probably not by Audley. It dates from before 1553. Since this section refers to the king's navy, it predates Mary's reign (1553–58). See C. S. L. Davis, "Naval Discipline in the Early Sixteenth Century," *Mariner's Mirror* 48 (1962): 223.

30. *Regulations and Instructions Relating to His Majesty's Service at Sea, Established by His Majesty in Council* (1731), p. 31, article 38.

31. *Regulations and Instructions* (1756), p. 200, article 11, "Rules for Preserving Cleanliness," item 5.

32. Ibid., items 1–4.

33. William Henry Dillon, *A Narrative of My Professional Adventures*, ed. Michael Lewis, 2 vols. (London: Navy Records Society, 1952), 1:96.

34. "Captain Richard G. Keats' Orders for H.M.S. *Superb*, 1803–1804," *Mariner's Mirror* 7 (1921): 317.

35. Robert Wauchope, *A Short Narrative of God's Merciful Dealings* (London: Privately printed, 1862), quoted in Evelyn Berckman, *The Hidden Navy* (London: Hamish Hamilton, 1973), 24–26.

36. *The Life, Journals, and Correspondence of Samuel Pepys*, ed. John Smith, 2 vols. (London: Richard Bentley, 1841), 1:111–12.

37. For two descriptions of payday, see Robinson, *Jack Nastyface*, 95–101, and John Harvey Boteler, *Recollections of My Sea Life from 1808 to 1830*, ed. David Bonner-Smith (London: Navy Records Society, 1942), 196–97.

38. Every man in a ship that captured an enemy vessel, or prize, received a share of the proceeds from the sale of the vessel and her cargo. The size of the share allotted was based on rank. Officers could grow rich on the percentage they got from a prize, while a seaman's share seldom amounted to more than a few pounds. Still, the hope of prize money loomed large in most seamen's dreams because of those very rare occasions when seamen had received a large amount. One of the greatest prizes was the

Spanish treasure ship *Hermione,* captured off Cadiz in 1762 by two British frigates; each captain got £65,000 and every seaman got £485, over twice the yearly wages of an ordinary seaman. Lloyd, *British Seaman,* 252–54.

39. "New Sea Song," in C. Harding Firth, ed., *Naval Songs and Ballads* (London: Navy Records Society, 1908), 239–40.

40. *Diary of Henry Teonge,* 36–38.

41. "The Sea-Martyrs; or, the Seamen's Sad Lamentation for Their Faithful Service, Bad Pay, and Cruel Usage," in Firth, *Naval Songs,* 141. For information on the *Suffolk* mutiny, see Narcissus Luttrell, *A Brief Historical Relation of State Affairs from September 1678 to April 1714,* 6 vols. (Oxford: Oxford University Press, 1857), 2:144.

42. Rodger, *Wooden World,* 134.

43. "Boscawen's Letters to His Wife, 1755–1756," in *The Naval Miscellany,* vol. 4, ed. Christopher Lloyd (London: Navy Records Society, 1952), 197. In the previous day's letter Boscawen noted that he was sending the money to the wives through his own private agent "Messrs. Child" (196). And in a letter from Plymouth dated 26 April 1755 he wrote, "You will like my west-country men that have been sent from Penzance, several of them have been with me today to desire me to send their wives their advance money, which I have done by the hand of Mr. Veale" (176–77).

44. The actual title of the act is "An Act for the Better Relief of the Poor of This Kingdom," 13 and 14 Car. 2, c. 12 (1662). It was better for the taxpayers, not for the poor.

45. *House of Commons Journals* 31 (1767): 248.

46. *The History of Portsmouth* (Portsmouth: J. C. Mottley, 1801), 93–94; "Order for Purchasing Houses and Making a Workhouse for the Poor of the Parish of Portsea" (1729), quoted in Robert East, ed., *Extracts from Records in the Possession of the Municipal Corporation of the Borough of Portsmouth* (Portsmouth: Henry Lewis, 1891), 737.

47. Richard Nicholls Worth, *History of Plymouth from the Earliest Period to the Present Time* (Plymouth: W. Brendon and Son, 1871), 198.

48. Llewellynn Jewitt, *A History of Plymouth* (London: Simpkins, Marshall; Plymouth: W. H. Luke, 1873), 610–11; Worth, *History of Plymouth,* 195–97.

49. Jewitt, *History of Plymouth,* 611 n.

50. Worth, *History of Plymouth,* 202.

51. From the Vagrancy Act of 1597 (39 Eliz. 1, c. 4) to the Vagrancy Act of 1792 (32 Geo. 3, c. 45), "rogues, vagabonds and sturdy beggars" were to be publicly whipped and then passed to their home parishes. See Sidney Webb and Beatrice Webb, *English Local Government: English Poor Law History, Part 1, The Old Poor Law* (London: Longmans, Green, and Co.,

1927), 351–55. According to the act of 1792, women were not to be publicly whipped, but there were cases of public whippings after that date. Flogging of women in private was not abolished until 1819 (59 Geo. 3, c. 12). See Webb and Webb, *English Local Government*, 382–83.

52. *Leeds Intelligencer*, 6 March 1787, quoted in ibid., 364–65 n. 4.

53. "Oh! Cruel," in Firth, *Naval Songs*, 324.

54. "The Seamen's Wives' Vindication," in ibid., 145.

55. Marriage Act: 26 Geo. 3, c. 33 (1754).

56. Alexander Keith, *Observations on the Act for Preventing Clandestine Marriages* (London, 1753), quoted in John Ashton, *The Fleet, Its River, Prison, and Marriages* (New York: Scribner and Welford, 1888), 359–60.

57. "Report of the Committee on Sir John Fielding's Plan for Preventing Burglaries and Robberies," *Parliamentary History* 16 (10 April 1770): 929.

58. Vagrancy Act: 3 Geo. 4, c. 40 (1822). The Vagrancy Act of 1744 (17 Geo. 2, c. 5), which was the basis for subsequent acts, divided vagrants into three categories. The least serious offenders were classed as "idle and disorderly"; next came "rogues and vagabonds," which included beggars; and last were "incorrigible rogues and vagabonds"—hardened criminals.

59. Vagrancy Act: 5 Geo. 4, c. 83 (1824).

60. A great deal has been written about the Contagious Diseases Acts. For a brief summary of their effects on prostitution in naval ports, see Rasor, *Reform in the Royal Navy*, 87–96. For Plymouth background, see Judith R. Walkowitz, *Prostitution and Victorian Society: Women, Class, and the State* (Cambridge: Cambridge University Press, 1980), 71–73, 153–67.

61. *An Address to the Officers of His Majesty's Navy by an Old Naval Surgeon* (Dublin: Curry, 1824), quoted in Lloyd and Coulter, *Medicine and the Navy*, 3:198. In the 1821 census the population of the parishes of Portsmouth, Portsea, and Alverstoke (including Gosport) totaled 55,990. *The Portsmouth Guide* (Portsmouth: Hollingsworth, 1828).

62. The census of 1821 lists 2,881 males to 4,388 females in Portsmouth and 17,544 males to 20,835 females for Portsea, for a combined total of 20,425 males to 25,223 females, or 4,798 more females than males. *Portsmouth Guide*.

63. Unpublished journal, "Samuel Stokes, 1806–1807 and 1809–1815: His Life in the Merchant and Royal Navies," excerpted in Henry Baynham, *From the Lower Deck: The Royal Navy, 1780–1840* (Barre, Mass.: Barre, 1970), 130.

64. Vagrancy Act: 17 Geo. 2, c. 5, sec. 9 and 28 (1744); orders of 1756 quoted in Webb and Webb, *English Local Government*, 367–68.

65. Quota Acts: 35 Geo. 3, c. 5 and 69 (1795). See Lloyd, *British Seaman*, 198–200.

66. *The Private Correspondence of Admiral Lord Collingwood,* ed. Edward Hughes (London: Navy Records Society, 1957), 86.
67. Lloyd and Coulter, *Medicine and the Navy,* 3:357.
68. Ronald Pearsall, *The Worm in the Bud: The World of Victorian Sexuality* (Toronto: Macmillan, 1969), 226.
69. A moistened vaginal sponge attached to a ribbon was suggested in *Practical Hints on How to Enjoy Life and Pleasure without Harm to Either Sex* (1826). Charles Knowlton (an American), in *The Fruits of Philosophy* (London: James Watson, 1834), suggested the use, within five minutes after coitus, of a douche of dissolved alum, or sulfate of zinc, or saleratus (sodium bicarbonate), or chloride of soda, or vinegar. Pearsall, *Worm in the Bud,* 215–16.
70. Lawrence Stone, *The Family, Sex, and Marriage in England, 1500–1800* (New York: Harper and Row, 1977), 537; Norman E. Himes, *Medical History of Contraception* (New York: Schocken, 1970), 195, 197–200. Himes quotes (188–90) the sixteenth-century Italian scientist Fallopio (for whom the Fallopian tubes are named), who in his book on syphilis urged the use of a linen sheath to prevent infection. Gabrielle Fallopio, *De morbo Gallico liber absolutismus* (Patavii [Batavia], 1546), 52.
71. Walkowitz, *Prostitution,* 214–15, 313 nn. 5 and 18.
72. Lester S. King, *The Medical World of the Eighteenth Century* (Chicago: University of Chicago Press, 1958), 313. King gives the ingredients of two medicines used to treat gonorrhea, which he found in a British (probably Scottish) dispensary ledger of 1787–88. The first, prescribed for a thirty-two-year-old woman, combined calomel, sugar of lead, white vitriol, crab's eyes, opium, and gum arabic; the second, for a fourteen-year-old girl, consisted of oil of sweet almonds and mucilage gum arabic, followed the next day by opium and extract of lead in gum arabic.
73. See Walkowitz, *Prostitution,* 152–55, 193–201. The social background of Plymouth prostitutes in the 1870s that Walkowitz describes was very similar to that of the prostitutes of Plymouth and Portsmouth in the eighteenth and early nineteenth centuries.
74. G. J. Marcus, *Heart of Oak: A Survey of British Sea Power in the Georgian Era* (London: Oxford University Press, 1975), 143–46; F. H. Edwards, *Crime and Law and Order in Mid-Victorian Portsmouth: The Portsmouth Papers No. 55* (Portsmouth: Portsmouth City Council, 1989), 3.
75. Henry Whitfeld, *Plymouth and Devonport in Times of War and Peace* (Plymouth: E. Chapple, 1900), 402, 405.
76. [Hawker], *Statement Respecting the Prevalence of Certain Immoral Practices,* 34 n.
77. Walkowitz, *Prostitution,* 306 n. 7.

78. Samuel Leech, *Six Years in a Man of War* (Boston: J. M. Whittemore, 1843), excerpted in Baynham, *From the Lower Deck*, 94; Robinson, *Jack Nastyface*, 89.

79. John Fielding, "Plan for Preserving Those Deserted Girls in This Town Who Become Prostitutes from Necessity," added to *An Account of the Origin and Effects of a Police Set on Foot by His Grace the Duke of Newcastle in the Year 1753 upon a Plan Presented to His Grace by the Late Henry Fielding, Esq.* (London: A. Millar, 1758), quoted in R. Leslie-Melville, *The Life and Work of Sir John Fielding* (London: Lincoln Williams, c. 1934), 123.

80. A pamphlet published by the Fund of Mercy (London, 1813) took the information from the *Times* (London) of 7 November 1812. Quoted in Ford K. Brown, *Fathers of the Victorians: The Age of Wilberforce* (Cambridge: Cambridge University Press, 1961), 25.

81. William Tait, *Magdalinism: An Inquiry into the Extent, Causes, and Consequences of Prostitution in Edinburgh* (Edinburgh: P. Rickard, 1840), 24.

82. Michael Pearson, *The Age of Consent* (Newton Abbot, Devon: David and Charles, 1972), 25.

83. George Pinckard, *Notes on the West Indies: Written during the Expedition under the Command of the Late General Sir Ralph Abercromby*, 3 vols. (London, 1806; reprint, Westport, Conn.: Negro Universities Press, 1970), 1:36–38.

84. Robert Mercer Wilson, "Remarks on Board His Majesty's Ship *Unité* of Forty Guns," in Henry George Thursfield, ed., *Five Naval Journals* (London: Navy Records Society, 1951), 131–32.

85. Brown, *Fathers of the Victorians*, 22.

86. Ibid., 329–40.

87. See Jewitt, *History of Plymouth*, 616–17; Walkowitz, *Prostitution*, 298 n. 28.

88. Between 1874 and 1877, of 1,310 prostitutes in Rescue Society homes, 1,080 had formerly been in domestic service. *Twenty-fifth Annual Report of the Rescue Society* (London, 1877), 14, cited in Walkowitz, *Prostitution*, 260 n. 13.

89. James Beard Talbot, *The Miseries of Prostitution* (London: James Madden, 1844), 69.

90. A handwritten note on the Admiralty library's copy of [Hawker], *Statement Respecting the Prevalence of Certain Immoral Practices Prevailing in His Majesty's Navy*, 2d ed. (London: J. Hatchard and Son, 1822), quoted in Lloyd and Coulter, *Medicine and the Navy*, 4:197.

91. [Hawker], *Statement Respecting the Prevalence of Certain Immoral Practices* (1821 ed.), 1.

92. Ibid., 39.
93. For a description of the way U. S. Navy officers also ignored homosexual incidents on board their ships see the autobiographical novel by Herman Melville, *White-Jacket; or, The World in a Man-of-War* (New York, 1850; reprint, New York: Grove, 1956), 353–54.
94. [Hawker] *Statement Respecting the Prevalence of Certain Immoral Practices* (1821 ed.), 27–28.
95. Ibid., 22.
96. Ibid., 34–35 n.
97. Anselm John Griffiths, *Observations on Some Points of Seamanship with Practical Hints on Naval Oeconomy* (Cheltenham, England: J. J. Hadley, Minerva, 1824), 43, 45, 46. On the matter of shore leave, Griffiths practiced what he preached; he had given shore leave to his men even during the late wars, and few deserted. Griffiths, *Impressment Fully Considered* (London: Norie, 1826), 158.
98. Griffiths, *Observations,* 49.
99. Ibid., 43–49.
100. *Regulations Established by the King in Council; and Instructions Issued by the Lords Commissioners of the Admiralty Relating to His Majesty's Service at Sea* (London: John Murray, 1826).
101. For information on the series of naval reforms from 1815 to the 1860s, see Lloyd, *British Seaman,* 271–84, and Michael Lewis, *The Navy in Transition, 1814–1864: A Social History* (London: Hodder and Stoughton, 1965).
102. David Hannay, "Odds and Ends of the Old Navy," *Mariner's Mirror* 4 (1914): 181.

CHAPTER 2

Women of the Lower Deck at Sea

Epigraph from ADM 1/432, Pellew to secretary of the Admiralty, dispatch from the *Queen Charlotte,* Algiers Bay, 28 August 1816.

1. In his anonymous pamphlet against the practice of permitting prostitutes on board naval ships, Admiral Edward Hawker claimed that in 1808 a captain took nine women common to the ship's company to sea; but Hawker got the information secondhand, and he failed to name either the ship or the captain. [Edward Hawker], *Statement Respecting the Prevalence of Certain Immoral Practices Prevailing in His Majesty's Navy* (London: Ellerton and Henderson, 1821), 9.

2. Thomas Walsingham (1360–1420), *Historia brevis* (London, 1574), quoted in Nicholas Harris Nicolas, *A History of the Royal Navy, from the Earliest Times to the Wars of the French Revolution,* 2 vols. (London: Richard Bentley, 1847), 2:265–66.

3. Nicolas, *History,* 2:280–84. Nicolas does not attribute the drowning of the women to the sailors' superstitious fears, but it seems obvious to me; otherwise it is hard to account for such an extreme action. This is the earliest example I have discovered of the superstition that a woman at sea brought forth deadly storms. It was prevalent by the seventeenth century. The closely related belief that female witches had power over the winds was found throughout Northern Europe from pre-Christian times. Pomponius Mela, writing around A.D. 40, noted that the Druids in Gaul believed in the power of women over the winds. Fletcher S. Bassett, *Legends and Superstitions of the Sea and Sailors* (Chicago: Belford, Clarke, 1885), 110. Even at the late date of 1969 there was concern that a visit by Britain's Princess Anne to a North Sea oil rig might bring on bad weather. Margaret Baker, *Folklore of the Sea* (Newton Abbot, Devon: David and Charles, 1979), 95.

4. *The Autobiography of Phineas Pett,* ed. W. G. Perrin (London: Navy Records Society, 1918), 163.

5. Admiralty journals, entry for 4 February 1674, Pepysian Library, Magdalene College, Oxford, quoted in J. R. Tanner, "A Fraud in the Navy," *Mariner's Mirror* 8 (1922): 148.

6. *Memoirs of Admiral the Right Honourable, the Earl of St. Vincent,* ed. Jedidiah Stephens Tucker, 2 vols. (London: Richard Bentley, 1844), 2:120.

7. *Regulations and Instructions Relating to His Majesty's Service at Sea* (1731), p. 31, article 38; *Regulations* (1808), p. 144, article 13.

8. John Harvey Boteler, *Recollections of My Sea Life from 1808 to 1830,* ed. David Bonner-Smith (London: Navy Records Society, 1942), 94–95.

9. ADM 1/5295, court-martial of Captain Marriot Arbuthnot of the *Guarland* "on several Articles exhibited against him by Mr. William Mackenzie, Purser of the said ship," 13 March 1755. The court ruled that the charges of misuse of the beer and water supply were "premeditated, malicious, frivolous and groundless...except the Eighteenth Article, namely carrying women to sea."

10. Collingwood to Purvis from the *Ocean,* 9 August 1808, in *The Private Correspondence of Admiral Lord Collingwood,* ed. Edward Hughes (London: Navy Records Society, 1957), 251–52.

11. Collingwood to W. W. Pole from the *Ville de Paris,* 1809, in ibid., 251 n. 2.

12. For information on the idlers, see Brian Lavery, *Nelson's Navy: The Ships, Men, and Organization, 1793–1815* (London: Conway Maritime Press, 1989), 195, 272–73. For the number of idlers and other ratings in various-sized vessels, see Michael Lewis, *A Social History of the Navy, 1793–1815* (London: George Allen and Unwin, 1960), 272.

13. For a detailed description of the two-watch system, see Lavery, *Nelson's Navy*, 194, 200–203. A few captains used a three-watch or even a four-watch system so that the men could sleep through the night. Admiral John Jervis used a three-watch system. Edward Pelham Brenton, *Life and Correspondence of John, Earl of St. Vincent*, 2 vols. (London: Henry Colburn, 1838), 1:145. A four-watch system is mentioned in George Watson, *Adventures of a Greenwich Pensioner* (Newcastle: R. T. Edgar, 1927), 70.

14. William Richardson, *A Mariner of England: An Account of the Career of William Richardson...[1780–1819] as Told by Himself*, ed. Spencer Childers (London: Conway Maritime Press, 1970), 171, 176.

15. G. J. Marcus, *Heart of Oak: A Survey of British Sea Power in the Georgian Era* (London: Oxford University Press, 1975), 224.

16. *Memoirs of the Earl of St. Vincent*, 1:193.

17. Ibid., 414.

18. Ibid.

19. The Wynne family came on board Captain Thomas Fremantle's ship the *Inconstant* on 24 June 1796, just three weeks before Jervis's 14 July memorandum complaining about the women of the lower deck. The Wynnes lived on board various ships of Jervis's fleet until the fall. Betsey Wynne noted in a journal entry of 29 July 1796, off Toulon on board the *Britannia*, "Nothing can express how kind, gallant and friendly the Admiral was to us [when the Wynnes had visited Jervis's flagship the *Victory*]. He said that he would wish us to stay in the Fleet all the summer, that when we were tired of Captain Foley [of the *Britannia*] we should go on board the *Victory*." *The Wynne Diaries, 1789–1890*, ed. Ann Fremantle, 3 vols. (London: Oxford University Press, 1935–40), vol. 2, *1794–1798*, 97–103, 212, 215–17.

20. Although both Nelson and Emma Hamilton acknowledged that Horatia was their child, Admiral Thomas Hardy, thirty years after Nelson's death, was still trying to save Nelson's reputation. He told an interviewer in 1835 the concocted story that Horatia was the daughter of the sailmaker of Nelson's ship the *Elephant* and that she was born on board during the Battle of Copenhagen, 2 April 1802. Hardy claimed that Nelson had taken a fancy to the baby and had sent her to Lady Hamilton to raise.

Dispatches and Letters of Vice Admiral Lord Viscount Nelson, ed. Nicholas Harris Nicolas, 7 vols. (London: Henry Colburn, 1844–46), 7:386.

21. Mary [Lacy] Slade, *The History of the Female Shipwright* (London: M. Lewis, 1773), 62.

22. Richardson, *Mariner of England,* 195.

23. Captain Frederick Marryat, who served in the navy between 1806 and 1815, gives a good description of skylarking in his novel *Jacob Faithful* (New York: D. Appleton, 1868), 361–62. In Cuthbert Collingwood's ship, on blockade off Cadiz in 1797, the men danced on the main deck to bag-pipes that members of the crew had made. This musical accompaniment ended, however, when rats ate the leather bellows. Collingwood to E. Blackett from the *Excellent,* 31 August 1797, in *A Selection from the Public and Private Correspondence of Vice-Admiral Lord [Cuthbert] Collingwood,* ed. G. L. Newnham Collingwood, 2 vols., 5th ed. (London: James Ridgway, 1837), 1:83–84.

24. Mordecai M. Noah, *Travels in England, France, Spain, and the Barbary States in the Years 1813, 14, and 15* (New York: Kirk and Mercein; London: John Miller, 1819), 11–14.

25. Henry Wadsworth, journal excerpt, 2 April 1803, in Dudley W. Knox, ed., *Naval Documents Related to the United States Wars with the Barbary Powers,* 2 vols. (Washington, D.C.: Government Printing Office, 1940), 2:387.

26. *Journal of Rear-Admiral Bartholomew James, 1752–1828,* ed. John Knox Laughton (London: Navy Records Society, 1896), 312.

27. Dudley Pope, *The Black Ship* (Philadelphia: J. B. Lippincott, 1964), 176–77.

28. A Spanish prisoner, taken by the *Diligence,* Captain Mends, reported that there were seven women on board the *Hermione* at the time of the mutiny, and that they were all murdered, but he was reporting from hearsay, and there is no substantiating evidence. David Hannay, *Naval Courts-Martial* (Cambridge: Cambridge University Press, 1914), 56.

29. Pope, *Black Ship,* 267.

30. ADM 1/5348, court-martial of Richard Redman [John Redmond], 13–15 March 1799.

31. William Henry Dillon, *A Narrative of My Professional Adventures, 1790–1839,* ed. Michael Lewis, 2 vols. (London: Navy Records Society, 1952–53), 2:329.

32. William O. S. Gilly, *Narratives of Shipwrecks in the Royal Navy between 1793 and 1849* (London: John W. Parker, 1850), 10–23.

33. Ibid., 15. Captain Wallis's official report of the wreck does not mention the newly impressed man's wife, nor does he include in the list of the

dead the names of the woman and child who died. *Naval Chronicle* 1 (1799): 333–35.

34. Richardson, *Mariner of England*, 169.

35. Ibid., 173, 176, 188.

36. Ibid., 196.

37. Admiralty ruling, 1751, in *The Barrington Papers, Selected from the Letters and Papers of Admiral the Honorable Samuel Barrington*, ed. D. Bonner-Smith, 2 vols. (London: Navy Records Society, 1937), 1:76–77. See also Lewis, *Social History*, 139–40, and Christopher Lloyd, *The British Seaman, 1200–1860: A Social Survey* (Rutherford, N.J.: Fairleigh Dickinson University Press, 1970), 69, 252.

38. *The Sergison Papers*, ed. Reginald Dundas Merriman (London: Navy Records Society, 1950), 210.

39. J. J. Keevil, Christopher Lloyd, and J. L. S. Coulter, *Medicine and the Navy, 1200–1900*, 4 vols., vols. 1 and 2 by Keevil, vols. 3 and 4 by Lloyd and Coulter (Edinburgh: E. and S. Livingstone, 1957–63), 3:60.

40. ADM 1/3597, 10 January 1703, quoted in Reginald Dundas Merriman, ed., *Queen Anne's Navy: Documents Concerning the Administration of the Navy of Queen Anne, 1702–1714* (London: Navy Records Society, 1957–63), 235 n. 1.

41. Report of Rear Admiral George Byng and David Furzer to the Admiralty, 24 January 1703, quoted in ibid., 234–35.

42. Supplementary order, 9 March 1703, cited in ibid., 235 n. 2.

43. British Library, Add. MSS. 9333, 29, 62, cited in J. J. Sutherland Shaw, "The Hospital Ship, 1608–1740," *Mariner's Mirror* 22 (1936): 422–26; Admiralty Library, Thomas Corbett, chief clerk, to the secretary of the Admiralty, 1719, "Naval Precedents," MSS., XIII, 69, cited in Merriman, *Queen Anne's Navy*, 219.

44. *Regulations and Instructions* (1731), p. 137, article 1; ADM 36/114, muster book, *Apollo*, 1747; ADM 36/1448, muster book, *Harwich*, 1749; wreck of the *Apollo* listed in Isaac Schomberg, *Naval Chronology*, 5 vols. (London: T. Edgerton, 1802), 5:9.

45. Garlick to Sick and Hurt Board, 8 October 1759, F/20, in-letters, 1742–65, National Maritime Museum, Greenwich, London, quoted in Lloyd and Coulter, *Medicine and the Navy*, 3:68.

46. Lloyd and Coulter, *Medicine and the Navy*, 4:63–64.

47. John Nicol, *The Life and Adventures of John Nicol, Mariner*, ed. John Howell (Edinburgh, 1822; reprint, New York: Farrar and Rinehart, 1936), 170.

48. The Turkish sultan, "The Grand Signior," to Mr. Smith, His Majesty's envoy at Constantinople, 8 September 1798, translation, *Naval Chronicle* 14 (1805): 472–73.

49. Nicol, *Life and Adventures,* 170–71.

50. ADM 36/14817, muster book, *Goliath,* 3 August–30 November 1798.

51. Christina White to Nelson, Nelson mss., Wellcome Historical Library, London, quoted in Christopher Lloyd, Notes, *Mariner's Mirror* 47 (1961): 301. See also Lloyd and Coulter, *Medicine and the Navy,* 3:147; ADM 36/12318, muster book, H.M.S. *Majestic,* 1 July–31 August 1798. The only seamen named White who was on board the *Majestic* at the Battle of the Nile was Thomas White from Stroudwater, Gloucestershire, who enlisted 1 July 1796 at age twenty-seven. He was not killed in the battle, nor did he die on board from his wounds. If he was indeed Christina White's husband, he died after being discharged.

52. Charles M'Pherson, *Life on Board a Man-of-War* (Glasgow: Blackie, 1829), excerpted in Henry Baynham, *From the Lower Deck: The Royal Navy, 1780–1840* (Barre, Mass.: Barre, 1970), 160.

53. Baynham, *From the Lower Deck,* 155.

54. Ibid., 161.

55. Edward Fraser, *The Enemy at Trafalgar* (New York: E. P. Dutton, 1906), 219–26; William Robinson, *Nautical Economy* (London: William Robinson, 1836), reprinted as *Jack Nastyface: Memoirs of a Seaman* (Annapolis: Naval Institute Press, 1973), 57–61. Robinson, who got his information by hearsay, reported that Jeannette, who had gone to sea to be with her husband, had joined the crew in disguise, but this seems unlikely.

56. Fraser, *Enemy at Trafalgar,* 227.

57. ADM 37/4810, muster book, H.M. Sloop *Swallow,* Commander Edward R. Sibly, 1 May–3 June 1812: Joseph Philan (Phelan), entered 1 April 1809, age twenty-four, from Waterford, Ireland, discharged dead, "one of eleven men slain in the fight with the enemy, 16 June 1812."

58. *Annual Register* 54 (1812): 93.

59. ADM 82/124, governors of Chatham Chest to the Admiralty, 11 August 1780.

60. ADM 82/124, list of persons admitted pensioners to the Chest at Chatham in September 1780: "Eleanor Moor: wound—a fracture on the cranium; ship—*Apollo;* when hurt—15 June 1780; annual pension—£4.0.0."

61. Edward H. Cree, *Naval Surgeon: The Voyages of Dr. Edward H. Cree, Royal Navy, as Related in His Private Journals, 1837–1856,* ed. Michael Levien (New York: E. P. Dutton, 1981), 36–119, esp. 40, 70, 79.

62. *Queen's Regulations and Admiralty Instructions for the Government of Her Majesty's Naval Service* (1879), p. 211, article 640.

63. W. B. Rowbotham, "The Naval General Service Medal, 1793–1840," *Mariner's Mirror* 23 (1937): 366–67.

64. Queen Victoria to Theodore Martin, 29 May 1870, quoted in Theodore Martin, *Queen Victoria as I Knew Her* (London: William Blackwood, 1908), 69–70. The letter also stated, "The Queen [she referred to herself in the third person] is most anxious to enlist everyone who can speak or write to join in checking this mad, wicked folly of 'Woman's Rights,' with all its attendant horrors on which her poor feeble sex is bent, forgetting every sense of womanly feeling and propriety."

65. Rowbotham, "Naval General Service Medal," 366, 360.

66. This was not the last time a woman was denied recognition for her service in the Royal Navy. In 1916 Kathleen Dyer joined H.M.S. *Calypso* as captain's servant, by Admiralty order, and she served for two and a half years. She was, however, refused the Naval War and Victory Medal that was given to all other ratings who served in the ship during that period. A. Macdermott, Answer to Query, *Mariner's Mirror* 25 (1939): 447.

CHAPTER 3
Women in Disguise in Naval Crews

Epigraph from John Ashton, ed., *Real Sailor-Songs* (London: Leadenhall, 1891), 60–61.

1. Anne Chamberlyne's monument was on the wall to the east of the south door. The church archives contain a transcription of the inscription from her monument, but the only memorial to her now on view is a recently embroidered kneeling stool depicting sailors and their ship and the inscription "Anne Spragg, 1667–1691, a Maiden Heroine, she fought as a sailor."

2. "Second Pallas" refers to Pallas Athena, the goddess of war. This translation, together with the Latin inscription, is found in Daniel Lysons, *Environs of London,* 2 vols., 2d ed. (London: T. Cadell and W. Davies, 1810), 2:68–70. See also *Survey of London* (London: London City Council, 1923), vol. 7, pt. 3, "Chelsea."

3. Thomas Faulkner, *An Historical and Topographical Description of Chelsea and Its Environs* (London: T. Egerton, 1810), 60–64.

4. Lysons, *Environs of London,* 2:81–82. See also the listing for Mary Astell, *Dictionary of National Biography.*

5. Narcissus Luttrell, *A Brief Historical Relation of State Affairs from September 1678 to April 1714,* 6 vols. (Oxford: Oxford University Press, 1857), 2:620.

6. ADM 51/3765, captain's log, *Amazon,* 1761.

7. ADM 36/4825, muster book, *Amazon,* 1 May–30 June 1761: "Wm. Prothero, Pte [private] entered 1 December 1760, discharged 30 April

1761, pr. Admty. Ord., slop cloaths, 16 shillings, 6 pence; tobacco 6 shillings, 4 pence."

8. J. C. Dickinson, "A Naval Diary of the Seven Years' War from Flookburgh," *Transactions of the Cumberland and Westmorland Antiquarian and Archaeological Society* 38 (1938): 241.

9. *Annual Register,* 1815, 64. There were a number of blacks in naval crews, including slaves sent to sea by their masters. Despite racial prejudice on land, it appears that blacks were usually accepted within the society of the lower deck. For the autobiography of a black slave in the eighteenth-century navy, see *The Interesting Narrative of the Life of Olaudah Equiano or Gustavus Vassa, the African...by Himself,* 2 vols. (London, 1789; reprint, New York: Negro University Press, 1969).

10. *Annual Register,* 1815, 64.

11. ADM 37/5680, muster book, *Queen Charlotte,* 31 December 1815–1 February 1816: "William Brown, AB, entered, 31 December, 1815, 1st Warrt., place of origin, Edinburgh, age, 32."

12. In that era a captain of the foretop or forecastle in a first-rate ship such as the *Queen Charlotte* earned approximately £2 6d. a month. See Brian Lavery, *Nelson's Navy: The Ships, Men, and Organization, 1793–1815* (London: Conway Maritime Press, 1989), 326, appendix 6 (chart of monthly pay in 1807).

13. ADM 37/5680, 31 December 1815–1 February 1816.

14. ADM 37/5680, 1 June–31 July 1816: "William Brown, AB, on 29 June 1816, entered the *Bombay,* late the *Trident*." (Vessels were often renamed.)

15. ADM 1/902, Cavendish to the Admiralty, 20 July 1739.

16. Ships' muster books, brought up to date about every two months, were often the only record of a man's service. The information was scanty: name, rank, date of hire, date of and reason for discharge, and occasionally a brief physical description. Sometimes a muster book also noted whether a man was pressed or a volunteer and gave the amount of any bounty he was paid. The navy was always careful about its money; specific items of clothing and tobacco purchased from the purser were always recorded and charged against future pay. By the nineteenth century more details were usually provided such as age upon entry and place and date of birth.

17. WO 116/4, Chelsea Hospital admission book, 14 February 1746–18 December 1754; *The Female Soldier; or, the Surprising Life and Adventures of Hannah Snell* (London: R. Walker, 1750), reprinted in Menie Muriel Dowie, ed., *Women Adventurers* (London: T. Fisher Unwin, 1893), 88–90. All subsequent citations to *The Female Soldier* refer to the Dowie reprint, pp. 55–131, which is more readily available than the 1750 edition.

18. John Curtin, "The Maiden Sailor," in Hyder Edward Rollins, ed., *The Pepys Ballads*, 8 vols. (Cambridge, Mass.: Harvard University Press, 1932), 6:176–77.
19. Quoted in Cyril Field, *Britain's Sea Soldiers* (Liverpool: Lyceum, 1924), 99 n.
20. Lewis [*sic*] de Bougainville, *A Voyage Round the World…in the Years 1766, 1767, 1768, and 1769*, trans. John Reinhold Forster (London, 1772; reprint, New York: Da Capo, 1967), 300.
21. Mary Slade, *The History of the Female Shipwright* (London: M. Lewis, 1773). The name of the author is given as Mary Slade, supposedly the married name of Mary Lacy. Since it is doubtful that she married, I have used her maiden name throughout this book.
22. *Annual Register*, 1807, 463.
23. Quoted in Field, *Britain's Sea Soldiers*, 99 n.
24. William Blackstone, *Commentaries on the Laws of England*, 4 vols. (Dublin: P. Byrne, 1796), 1:468.
25. E. P. Thompson, *Customs in Common* (London: Merlin, 1991), 409.
26. See the chapter "Sale of Wives," in ibid., 404–66. See also Samuel P. Menefee, *Wives for Sale* (New York: St. Martin's; Oxford: B. Blackwell, 1981).
27. *Annual Register*, 1766, 75.
28. In the end Alexander retreated from his daring position, adding a disclaimer to his exposition, suggesting that, after all, women were content with their lack of independence: "Thus excluded from everything which can give them consequence, they derive the greater part of the power which they enjoy from their charms; and these, when joined to sensibility, often fully compensate in this respect." William Alexander, *The History of Women from the Earliest Antiquity to the Present Time*, 2 vols. (London: W. Strahan and T. Cadell, 1782), 2:505–6.
29. *Annual Register*, 1761, 170.
30. *Naval Chronicle* 17 (January–June 1807): 309.
31. Dowie, *Women Adventurers*, 97–98.
32. Slade, *Female Shipwright*, preface, iv.
33. Curtin, "Maiden Sailor," 176–77.
34. Examples of ballads based on the lost-lover theme are found in almost any extensive collection of ballads in the English and Scottish tradition. For twentieth-century Canadian versions, see Helen Creighton, ed., *Songs and Ballads from Nova Scotia* (Toronto, 1933; reprint, New York: Dover, 1966), "Caroline and Her Young Sailor Bold," "Female Sailor Bold," "Rose of Britain's Isle," and "Billy Taylor"; and MacEdward Leach, ed., *Folk Ballads and Songs of the Lower Labrador Coast* (Ottawa: National

Museum of Canada, 1965), "Caroline and Her Young Sailor Bold," "Willy Taylor," "The Sailor Boy," and "The Lady and the Sailor." For an analysis, largely differing from mine, of female-warrior ballads, see Dianne Dugaw, *Warrior Women and Popular Balladry, 1650–1850* (Cambridge: Cambridge University Press, 1989).

35. "The Marchants Daughter of Bristow," pt. 1, in *A Collection of Seventy-nine Black Letter Ballads and Broadsides Printed in the Reign of Queen Elizabeth, between the Years 1559 and 1597* (London: Joseph Lilly, 1867), 66–77.

36. John Ashton, ed., *Modern Street Ballads* (London: Chatto and Windus, 1888), 254–55.

37. *Annual Register*, 1771, 71.

38. Dowie, *Women Adventurers*, 64–67.

39. The two editions of the original biography, of 46 and 187 pages, respectively, have the same title, publisher, and date: *The Female Soldier; or, the Surprising Life and Adventures of Hannah Snell* (London: R. Walker, 1750). The longer version, with some abbreviated passages, is the one reprinted in Dowie, *Women Adventurers*, 54–131. An account of Snell appeared in *Gentleman's Magazine*, vol. 20, in July 1750, the same month the biography was published, and was picked up by other periodicals. The biography has been reprinted in various forms over the years in both England and the United States. These include *The Female Soldier* (London: William and Cluer Dicey, 1756); *The Female Warrior; or, Surprising Life and Adventures of Hannah Snell* (London: Wilmott and Hill, 1801); *The Surprising Life and Adventures of Hannah Snell* (York: J. Kendrew, 1809); and *The Widow in Masquerade* (Northampton, Mass., 1809). A facsimile edition of the shorter version of the 1750 biography was recently published with an introduction by Dianne Dugaw (Los Angeles: William Andrews Clark Memorial Library, University of California, 1989). Dugaw is primarily concerned with comparing Snell's story with ballads about female warriors. She accepts the lost-lover theme as Snell's motive for joining the army. She does not, in fact, question the veracity of any part of the biography.

 Snell's story appeared in numerous collections, including *Kirby's Wonderful and Scientific Museum; or, Magazine of Remarkable and Eccentric Characters* (London: R. S. Kirby, 1804), 2:430–38; *Eccentric Biography; or, Memoirs of Remarkable Female Characters* (Worcester, Mass.: Isaiah Thomas, 1804), 295–307; John Timbs, *English Eccentrics and Eccentricities* (London: Chatto and Windus, 1875), 116–21; Ellen Creathorne Clayton, *Female Warriors*, 2 vols. (London: Tinsley Brothers, 1879), 2:16–23; John Ashton, *Eighteenth Century Waifs* (London: Hurst and Blackett, 1887), 185–90; and John Laffin, *Women in Battle* (London and New York: Abelard Schuman, 1967). The *Dictionary of National Biography,* 613, is the only source that casts doubt on the veracity of Snell's biography. It states, "The bombastic opening…, the impossible incidents of the floggings"—it was claimed that she received five hundred lashes in the army, a number that usually proved fatal, and then, without any time to recover, proceeded to walk several hundred miles—"and the circumstantial account of the last moments of Hannah's criminal husband all attest the workmanship of an experienced literary hand, to whose identity no clue exists."

40. WO 116/4, Wednesday, 21 November 1750, Chelsea Hospital admission book, covering period from 14 February 1746 to 18 December 1754; affidavit by Hannah Snell, dated 27 June 1750, in Dowie, *Women Adventurers,* 57. In this affidavit, reproduced in her biography, Snell swore before J. Blachford, the lord mayor of the City of London, that the experiences listed in the affidavit were true, and she signed it with an X (her mark). Her sister Susannah Gray was a witness. The affidavit lists Snell's date and place of birth and the vessels she served in. It is noteworthy that the fictional material of the biography is not included in the affidavit; there is, for example, no mention of Snell's Dutch husband James Summs.

41. There is a gap in Snell's history. The affidavit says that she joined the army on 27 November 1745. The biography reports that she was discharged after about four months, spent a month walking to Portsmouth, remained in Portsmouth for a month before she joined the marines, and went on board the *Swallow* three weeks later. According to this schedule, she would have joined the *Swallow* around June 1746. The muster book of the *Swallow,* however, states that she came on board on 24 October 1747. Approximately a year and four months is unaccounted for. See Dowie, *Women Adventurers,* 70–71; ADM 36/3472, muster book, sloop *Swallow.*

42. ADM 36/3472, muster book, sloop *Swallow;* WO 116/4, 21 November 1750, Chelsea Hospital admission book, 1746–54, "Wounded at Pondicherry in the thigh of both leggs"; Dowie, *Women Adventurers,* 87–90.

43. ADM 36/1035, muster book, H.M.S. *Eltham:* "Jae. Gray [released] Cudelore Hopl. 2 Aug 1749, rec'd [into the *Eltham*] from *Tartar* 13 Oct. 1749."

44. ADM 36/1035, muster book, H.M.S. *Eltham,* Jae. Gray, discharged 25 May 1750, Spithead, "per order of Adml. Hawke."

45. Dowie, *Women Adventurers,* 127.

46. Ibid., 123.

47. Ibid., 124–27; "'A New Song' sung by Hannah Snell, alias James Gray, at the New Wells, Goodman's Fields." Broadside in the Madden Collection, Cambridge, *Slipsongs*, 2:333, no. 1406, quoted in Charles Harding Firth, ed., *Naval Songs and Ballads* (London: Navy Records Society, 1908), 200. It focused on the romantic crowd-rousers—love and glory, patriotism, and the lost-lover motif, and was based on a popular ballad about Susan and her sweetheart William. The following verses give the gist of Snell's song:

All ye noble British spirits that midst dangers glory sought,
  Let it lessen not your merit that a woman bravely fought:
Cupid slyly first enroll'd me, Pallas next her force did bring,
  Press'd my heart to venture boldly for my love and for my King.

Sailor-like to fear a stranger, straight I ventured on the main,
  Facing death and every danger, love and glory to obtain.
Tell me, you who hear my story, what could more my courage move?—
  [King] George's name inspired with glory, William was the man I loved.

When from William Susan parted, she but wept and shook her hand;
  I, more bold (tho' tender-hearted), left my friends and native land;
Bravely by his side, maintaining British rights, I shed my blood,
  Still to him unknown remaining, watch'd to serve and do him good.

In the midst of blood and slaughter, bravely fighting for my king,
  Facing death from every quarter, fame and conquest home to bring.
Sure you'll own 'tis more than common, and the world proclaim it, too.
  Never yet did any woman more for love and glory do.

48. WO 116/4, Chelsea Hospital admission book, 1746–54.
49. Dowie, *Women Adventurers,* 129. According to records at the Greater London Record Office, no license was issued to Hannah Snell or James Gray in or near Wapping between 1750 and 1758. "Licensed Victuallers Registers and Recognizancies" and "Register of the Inn-keepers, Alehouse-keepers, e.c. within the Tower Division" (includes the Thames-side parishes: Wapping, Wapping Wall, Limehouse, Poplar, etc.), 1750–58.
50. *Universal Chronicle,* 3–10 November 1759, 359; Lysons, *Environs of London,* 2:99–100; Timbs, *English Eccentrics,* 121; *Dictionary of National Biography,* 613–14.
51. *Times* (London), 4 November 1799, quoted in John Ashton, *Old Times: A Picture of Social Life at the End of the Eighteenth Century* (London: John C. Nimmo, 1885), 94.

52. For the 1804 Kirby volume, see note 39. The *Times* reported that "she personated a common sailor before the mast, during a cruise in the North Seas." (There is no such cruise in the autobiography.) The *Times* goes on to say that after a lovers' quarrel Talbot left the navy "and assumed for a time the military character" but returned to the navy and was wounded in the battles of Cape St. Vincent (14 February 1797) and Camperdown (11 October 1797). The autobiography says that she received her wounds at the Glorious First of June, 1794, three years earlier.

53. *The Life and Surprising Adventures of Mary Anne Talbot* (London: Robert S. Kirby, 1809), reprinted in Dowie, *Women Adventurers*, 133–96.

54. Most of the collections of biographies that include Talbot also include Hannah Snell; for example, Clayton, Dowie, Ashton, and Laffin (listed in note 39). An exception is the version in the 1804 collection *Eccentric Biography*, which is based on the 1799 *Times* interview. The *Dictionary of National Biography*, which devotes over a column to Talbot, expresses vague doubt of the story's authenticity, although it states, "The nucleus of her tale…is probably true."

55. Dowie, *Women Adventurers*, 139. As with Snell's biography, I have cited Dowie's reprint of Talbot's autobiography rather than Kirby's 1809 edition because it is more readily available.

56. Ibid., 143.

57. Records of Regimental Headquarters, Queen's Lancashire Regiment, Warrington, Cheshire; David Syrett et al., *The Commissioned Sea Officers of the Royal Navy, 1660–1815* (London: Scolar Press for Navy Records Society, 1994), 44: Essex Bowen was commissioned lieutenant, 28 February 1758; superannuated commander, 11 August 1798; died July 1811.

58. The Eighty-second Regiment of Foot had been disbanded in 1784 and was not reformed until autumn 1793. The Eighty-second Regiment remained in England until embarking for Gibraltar 31 August 1794, and they sailed from there to St. Domingo in 1795. Records of Regimental Headquarters, Queen's Lancashire Regiment; ADM 36/11014, muster book, *Crown* transport, 1 March–31 May 1792.

59. ADM 36/11176, muster book, *Brunswick*, March–April 1794. The only John Taylor on board at the battle of the Glorious First of June, 1794, was a fourteen-year-old captain's servant who had entered at Portsmouth 18 December 1793 and was discharged by request, together with his brother Isaac, on 4 July 1794. He was not wounded in the battle.

60. ADM 36/11176, muster book, *Brunswick*, June–July 1794; ADM 102/274, muster book, Haslar Hospital, June–July 1794.

61. ADM 36/12698, muster book, *Vesuvius*, Captain Thomas Rogers, 1793–95.

62. *Lloyd's Register*, 1796: schooner *Ariel*, J. Field (captain), 137 tons, New York to London, American registry.
63. Dowie, *Women Adventurers*, 181–82.
64. *Annual Register*, 1771, 71.
65. Newspaper account quoted in Frank George Griffith Carr, "Women and the Sea from the Days of Genesis," *The Wren*, June 1953, 6.
66. Ibid.
67. *Annual Register*, 1782, 221.
68. Deuteronomy 22:5: "A woman shall not wear that which pertaineth to a man, neither shall a man put on a woman's garment; for whosoever doeth such things is an abomination unto Jehovah thy God."
69. St. Jerome, *Commentaries: Epistolam ad Ephesios*, 3.5.658, quoted in Vern L. Bullough, *Sexual Variance in Society and History* (New York: John Wiley and Sons, 1976), 365.
70. Most of the legendary female transvestite saints became monks, and often they were discovered to be women only after their deaths. See *Butler's Lives of the Saints*, ed. Herbert Thurston and Donald Attwater, 4 vols. (New York: P. J. Kenedy and Sons, 1956), St. Pelagia, 4:59–61; St. Athanasia, 4:60–70; St. Apollinaris, 1:33; St. Eugenia, 4:612; St. Euphrosyne, 1:4–5; and St. Anastasia Patricia, 2:546–47.
71. Nell Gwyn, the mistress of Charles II (1660–85), played breeches roles, and so did Mrs. Jordan, the popular actress who lived happily with the duke of Clarence and bore him ten children. He became King William IV (1830–37). See Vern L. Bullough, *Sin, Sickness, and Society* (New York: New American Library, 1977), 79.
72. William Wycherley, *The Plain Dealer* (London: Thomas Newcomb, for James Magnes and Richard Bentley, 1677). There are many recent reprints, including one published by the University of Nebraska Press (Lincoln, 1967) and a facsimile of the 1677 edition (Yorkshire: Scholar Press, 1971).
73. John Mitford, *The Adventures of Johnny Newcome in the Navy* (London: Sherwood, Neely, and Jones, 1819), 264 n. 134.
74. The scholarly seven-volume slang dictionary *Slang and Its Analogues*, ed. John S. Farmer and W. E. Henley (London, 1890–1904; one-volume reprint, New York: Arno, 1970) defines *lesbian* as "a fellatrix of women." The 1878–1928 edition of the *Oxford English Dictionary* includes the word *tribade* while excluding *lesbian*. Its definition of *tribade* reflects the prejudice of its time: "A woman who practices unnatural vice with other women."
75. Romans 1:26–27: "For this cause God gave them up unto vile passions for their women changed the natural use unto that which is against

nature; and likewise also the men, leaving the natural use of the woman, burned in their lust, one toward another, men with men working unseemliness."

76. Slade, *Female Shipwright*, 191.

77. Quoted in John Ashton, *The Fleet, Its River, Prison, and Marriages* (New York: Scribner and Welford, 1888), 382.

78. *Annual Register*, 1777, 191.

79. *Annual Register*, 1760, 84–85.

80. Ibid.

81. Ibid.

82. Statute 2 Henry 8, c. 6 (1533) made sodomy a capital offense for both parties, if both were over fourteen. In 1820 most of the two hundred capital crimes that had been on the books in the later eighteenth century were reduced, but sodomy remained a capital crime until 1861, although there were few convictions that drew the death penalty after 1830.

83. Articles of War, Article 29, Navy Act: Statute 22 Geo. 2, c. 33 (1749).

84. "The Revelations to the Monk of Evesham (Abbey)," in Edward Arber, ed., *English Reprints*, 8 vols. (London: English Reprints, 1869), 8:58–59.

85. Edward Coke, *The Third Part of the Institutes of the Laws of England* (London, 1644; reprint, London: W. Clarke and Sons, 1817), cap. 10, "Of Buggery or Sodomy," 58–59.

86. Blackstone, *Commentaries on the Laws of England*, 4:215–16.

87. Thomas Pasley, *Private Sea Journals, 1778–1783* (London: J. M. Dent and Sons, 1931), 215, 227.

88. *Naval Chronicle* 18 (July–December 1807): 342.

89. *Annual Register*, 1807, 463.

90. ADM 36/17099, muster book, *Hazard*, 1807; *Annual Register*, 1807, 463.

91. *Annual Register*, 1807, 463.

92. ADM 1/5383, court-martial of William Berry, first lieutenant of H.M. Sloop *Hazard*, on board His Majesty's Ship *Salvador del Mundo* in Hamoaze, second day of October 1807, and by adjournment the third of the same month, "for an unnatural crime."

93. Statutes 5 Eliz. 1, c. 17 (1562) and 22 Geo. 2, c. 33, s. 2 and 29 (1749). If the victim was under fourteen, the age of discretion for males, he was innocent; if both participants were over fourteen, it was a felony for both. See also Blackstone, *Commentaries on the Laws of England*, 4:216, and Leon Radzinowicz, *A History of English Criminal Law and Its Administration from 1750*, 5 vols. (London: Stevens and Sons, 1948), 1:632.

94. ADM 1/5383, court-martial of William Berry.

95. Ibid.; *Naval Chronicle* 18 (July–December 1807): 342–43.

96. Anne Jane Thornton, passing as a man, served in several merchant vessels including the *Sarah,* Captain McIntire, of Belfast, in which she worked as cook and steward around 1835. *Annual Register,* 1835, 24–26; *Interesting Life and Wonderful Adventures of That Extraordinary Woman Anne Jane Thornton, the Female Sailor* (London: J. Thompson, 1835). Her name was used in a nineteenth-century ballad, "The Female Sailor Bold," a version of which was still being sung in the 1930s, but it erroneously placed her adventures in 1865. Creighton, *Songs and Ballads from Nova Scotia,* 96–97.

In 1848 Ann Johnson, under the name of George Johnson, served in the American whaling ship *Christopher Mitchell,* Captain Thomas Sullivan, for a period of seven months. Elizabeth A. Little, "The Female Sailor on the *Christopher Mitchell:* Fact and Fantasy," *American Neptune* 54 (Fall 1994): 252–56. Georgiana Leonard shipped as George Welden in the whaling bark *America,* Captain John A. Luce, from New Bedford, on 15 November 1862. Her gender was revealed on 9 January 1863, when she was ordered to be flogged for having attacked the second mate with a knife. Suzanne J. Stark, "The Adventures of Two Women Whalers," *American Neptune* 44 (Winter 1984): 22–24.

CHAPTER 4

The Story of Mary Lacy, Alias William Chandler

Epigraph from the oral tradition.

1. Mary Slade, *The History of the Female Shipwright; to Whom the Government Has Granted a Superannuated Pension of Twenty Pounds per Annum, during Her Life: Written by Herself* (London: M. Lewis, 1773), 191 pages. The preface is signed M. Slade, the surname being that of the man Lacy claimed to have married after she retired from the navy.

2. Mary Lacy, *The Female Shipwright; or, Life and Extraordinary Adventures of Mary Lacy... Written by Herself* (New York: Printed for George Sinclair by J. C. Totten, 1807), 35 pages; Mary Lacy, *The Life and Extraordinary Adventures of Mary Lacy,* printed and bound with *The Life, Travels, Voyages, and Daring Engagements of the Celebrated [John] Paul Jones* (New York: Printed for E. Duyckinck...by G. Bunce, c. 1809), Lacy section, 54 pages; Mary Lacy of Wickham, Kent, England, *The Female Shipwright; or, Life and Extraordinary Adventures of Mayr* [sic] *Lacy... Written by Herself* (Philadelphia: William M'Carty, publisher, Ann Coles, printer, 1814), 35 pages.

3. Henry Robert Plomer, *A Dictionary of the Printers and Booksellers Who Were at Work in England, Scotland, and Ireland from 1726 to 1775* (Oxford: Oxford University Press, 1930), 155. Plomer identifies Lewis as a publisher of religious pamphlets for groups such as the Moravians (the United Brethren) and gives as an example the Rev. A. M. Toplady's attack on John Wesley, *An Old Fox Tarr'd and Feathered,* which Lewis published in 1775. A manifestation of the Moravians' wealth was their ownership of Lindsey House, a splendid mansion on fashionable Cheyne Walk in Chelsea, London, bought for them in 1750 by their leader, Count Nicholas Zinzendorf. Patrick O'Brian, *Joseph Banks: A Life* (Boston: David R. Godine, 1993), 31.

4. It was a common practice in mid-eighteenth-century charity and workhouse schools to put the children to work producing salable items for the profit of the institution. Many of these schools were little better than sweatshops. Phyllis Stock, *Better Than Rubies: A History of Women's Education* (New York: G. P. Putnam's Sons, 1978), 71–72. While Lacy's schoolmistress slighted reading and writing in favor of household skills, she at least gave Lacy some of the profits of her labor. Girls in charity schools were taught only a little reading and even less writing and arithmetic, far less than boys, because while poor boys might go into a trade, girls were destined for domestic service, where literacy was not required.

5. ADM 36/6767, muster book, *Sandwich,* April–October 1759. On 10 April 1759, at Chatham, wages began for the warrant officers and the few seamen already on board.

6. For background information on the Seven Years' War and the role played by the *Sandwich,* see William Laird Clowes, *The Royal Navy: A History from the Earliest Times to the Present,* 7 vols. (London: Sampson Low, Marston, 1897–1903), vol. 3, *1714–1793,* 216–38; Julian Stafford Corbett, *England in the Seven Years War,* 2 vols. (London: Longmans, Green, 1907), vol. 2; Ruddock F. Mackay, *Admiral Hawke* (Oxford: Clarendon, 1965), chaps. 12–17; Geoffrey J. Marcus, *Quiberon Bay* (Barre, Mass.: Barre, 1963); G. J. Marcus, *A Naval History of England: The Formative Centuries* (Boston: Little, Brown, 1961), chaps. 10–11; and *The Barrington Papers, Selected from the Letters and Papers of Admiral the Honorable Samuel Barrington,* ed. D. Bonner-Smith, 2 vols. (London: Navy Records Society, 1937), vol. 1.

7. ADM 36/6767, April–October 1759; ADM 36/6768, October 1759–March 1760; ADM 36/6769, March–October 1760; and ADM 36/6770, October 1760–December 1761, muster books, *Sandwich,* list William Russel, gunner, and Jeremiah Paine, his servant.

8. ADM 36/6767 lists "Richard Baker and William Chandler, his servant, entered 9 May 1759." ADM 36/6768 and ADM 36/6769 also list them.

Chandler was discharged from the *Sandwich* 30 March 1761. ADM 36/6770.

9. At Black Stakes, a reach of the Medway a short distance above Sheerness, ships from Chatham took in their guns and completed fitting for sea. It is not on modern charts. Reginald Dundas Merriman, ed., *Queen Anne's Navy: Documents Concerning the Administration of the Navy of Queen Anne, 1702–1714* (London: Navy Records Society, 1961), 108.

10. In May 1759, as Sir Edward Hawke gathered his squadron together for the blockade of Brest and other ports on the Atlantic coast of France, he found there was a severe shortage of seamen in the ships of the line. On 13 May, therefore, he ordered that sixteen hundred men be transferred into the large ships from his frigates, sloops, and other smaller vessels. Mackay, *Admiral Hawke,* 201.

11. Admiral Geary, who had just been promoted rear admiral in June, was third in command under Hawke; Vice Admiral Sir Charles Hardy was second in command. Marcus, *Quiberon Bay,* 34 n. Richard Norbury was captain of the *Sandwich.*

12. "Qui voit Ouessant voit son sang." Nigel Calder, *The English Channel* (New York: Viking, Penguin, 1986), 9.

13. ADM 36/6767; "Biographical Memoir of the Late Sir Francis Geary, Bart.," *Naval Chronicle* 17 (1807): 182; Mackay, *Admiral Hawke,* 228.

14. Marcus, *Quiberon Bay,* 112 (quoting from ADM I/92, 13 October 1759).

15. Ibid., 131–33.

16. Ibid., 133.

17. Ibid., 140 (from ADM I/93, 15 November 1759).

18. Ibid., 141 (from ADM I/93, 16 November 1759).

19 Mackay, *Admiral Hawke,* 260–61.

20. Ibid., 261 (from ADM I/93, 26 December 1759).

21. At this time Admiral Edward Boscawen (in the *Royal William*) was in charge of the squadron, with Geary (in the *Sandwich*) second in command. Together with other ships including the *Ramillies*, ninety guns, until recently Hawke's flagship, they were headed for Quiberon Bay when the hurricane struck. Boscawen noted that "it blew stronger than I ever felt in my life." The *Ramillies* was wrecked on the section of the Devon coast where the *Sandwich* had spent such a parlous night on 11 November, three months before. The captain of the *Ramillies*, Wittewronge Taylor, all his officers, and seven hundred men were lost; only one midshipman and (as Lacy reports) twenty-five of the crew were saved. Clowes, *Royal Navy,* 3:231; Mackay, *Admiral Hawke,* 265.

22. Lacy does not name the hospital—she only says that she was put in "the fifth ward south"—but obviously it was Haslar, the huge naval hospital in Gosport, still a major facility today. I could not verify her stay, since

there is no muster for Haslar for that period. The treatment of bleeding, although a dangerous one, was welcomed by Lacy; she reports that she received the bloodletting "with great relief."

23. Although Lacy worked as a supernumerary in the *Royal Sovereign* beginning in the autumn of 1760, she was not listed in that ship's muster until 1762. As William Chandler, she remained on the muster books of the *Sandwich* as Baker's servant until 30 March 1761, when she was discharged "by request." ADM 36/6768, October 1759–April 1760; ADM 36/6769, April–October 1760; and ADM 36/6770, October 1760–April 1761. It was not unusual for a man to work temporarily in a different vessel from his own until he could rejoin her and, meantime, to continue on the muster of his own ship. Lacy says she was a purser's servant in the *Royal Sovereign* in 1762; the muster books for that year list William Chandler as captain's servant. ADM 36/6799 and ADM 36/6800.

24. Geary came to the *Royal Sovereign* in the autumn of 1760. "Biographical Memoir of…Geary," *Naval Chronicle* 17 (1807): 184.

25. ADM 36/6798, ADM 36/6799, and ADM 36/6800, muster books, *Royal Sovereign,* 1762, list Robert Dawkins, boatswain.

26. The word *accompts* is an obsolete form of *accounts;* that is, she was taught accounting procedures.

27. Compared with the starting age in other apprenticeships, sixteen was a late beginning for a seven-year stint. It meant that shipwright status could not be attained before the age of twenty-three. (The entrance age was lowered to fifteen in 1765 and to fourteen in 1769.) Lacy was twenty-three when she entered and thirty when she became a shipwright. N. Macleod, "The Shipwrights of the Royal Dockyards," *Mariner's Mirror* 11 (1925): 286.

28. ADM 42/1100, muster book, *Royal William,* April–June 1763, lists Alexander McLean, carpenter, and his servant William Chandler. Apprentices were referred to as servants. Macleod, "Shipwrights," 286.

29. Shipwrights were paid 2s. 1d. a day. Chips money added a few pence. Shipwrights did very heavy work tearing up as well as building ships, so a twelve-hour day with four or five hours of overtime added on was very tiring indeed. They were supposed to be paid quarterly, but pay was always at least one quarter in arrears, often several quarters. Macleod, "Shipwrights," 286.

30. The fire destroyed a large number of the dockyard buildings and the "fitted rigging of 23 ships in ordinary." Jonathan G. Coad, *The Royal Dockyards, 1690–1850,* for the Royal Commission on the Historical Monuments of England (Aldershot, Hants: Scolar, Gower, 1989), 133,

quoting from a letter from Portsmouth Dockyard: Commissioner Hughes to the Admiralty, ADM/B/183, 27 July 1770.

31. ADM 3/79, Admiralty minute book, 28 January 1772, 78–79. Present: earl of Sandwich, Mr. Buller, Lord Lisburne.

32. Answer from B.G.C. to Query 83, "A Woman Shipwright," *Mariner's Mirror* 6 (1920): 350.

33. I was unable to find a certificate of this marriage, but records are far from complete for that period. There was no central file of marriages until 1837, when the Registration and Marriage Acts of 1836 came into operation. Before that each Church of England parish kept its own records.

34. Clowes, *Royal Navy*, 3:326; Coad, *Royal Dockyards,* 133; David Lyon, *The Sailing Navy List: All the Ships of the Royal Navy—Built, Purchased, and Captured—1688–1860* (London: Conway Maritime Press, 1993), 8.

INDEX

Ship names appear in italic type and, unless otherwise identified, are Royal Navy vessels.

ABOUT THE AUTHOR

SUZANNE J. STARK is an editor, lecturer, and freelance writer whose work has appeared in leading maritime journals. She has a degree in art history and has painted and exhibited in Amsterdam, New York, and San Francisco. She has worked as a textbook editor and writer for Houghton Mifflin, Harcourt Brace, and other publishers. She now lives on Beacon Hill in Boston, Massachusetts.

The **Naval Institute Press** is the book-publishing arm of the U.S. Naval Institute, a private, nonprofit society for sea service professionals and others who share an interest in naval and maritime affairs. Established in 1873 at the U.S. Naval Academy in Annapolis, Maryland, where its offices remain, today the Naval Institute has more than 85,000 members worldwide.

Members of the Naval Institute receive the influential monthly magazine *Proceedings* and discounts on fine nautical prints and on ship and aircraft photos. They also have access to the transcripts of the Institute's Oral History Program and get discounted admission to any of the Institute-sponsored seminars offered around the country.

The Naval Institute also publishes *Naval History* magazine. This colorful bimonthly is filled with entertaining and thought-provoking articles, first-person reminiscences, and dramatic art and photography. Members receive a discount on *Naval History* subscriptions.

The Naval Institute's book-publishing program, begun in 1898 with basic guides to naval practices, has broadened its scope in recent years to include books of more general interest. Now the Naval Institute Press publishes about 100 titles each year, ranging from how-to books on boating and navigation to battle histories, biographies, ship and aircraft guides, and novels. Institute members receive discounts of 20 to 50 percent on the Press's nearly 600 books in print.

For a free catalog describing Naval Institute Press books currently available, and for further information about subscribing to *Naval History* magazine or about joining the U.S. Naval Institute, please write to:

Membership Department
U.S. Naval Institute
118 Maryland Avenue
Annapolis, Maryland 21402-5035

Telephone: (800) 233-8764
Fax: (410) 269-7940